A Schoolboy's Wartime Letters

A Schoolboy's Wartime Letters

Geoffrey Iley

Winchester, UK
Washington, USA

First published by Chronos Books, 2014
Chronos Books is an imprint of John Hunt Publishing Ltd., Laurel House, Station Approach, Alresford, Hants, SO24 9JH, UK
office1@jhpbooks.net
www.johnhuntpublishing.com

For distributor details and how to order please visit the 'Ordering' section on our website.

Text copyright: Geoffrey Iley 2013

ISBN: 978 1 78279 504 9

A CIP catalogue record for this book is available from the British Library.

Design: Stuart Davies
www.stuartdaviesart.com

Printed and bound by CPI Group (UK) Ltd, Croydon, CR0 4YY

We operate a distinctive and ethical publishing philosophy in all areas of our business, from our global network of authors to production and worldwide distribution.

CONTENTS

To Norman and Winnie Iley — also to R.V. Rigby
and G. Talbot-Griffith.
Two wonderful parents and two remarkable, dynamic and
dedicated headmasters.

Acknowledgements

Photographs are from the author's album with the following exceptions:

Pictures numbered 5, 7 and 8 by kind permission of G.F. Wilson.

Picture number 6 by kind permission of Oakham School Foundation.

Year One

Autumn 1939 — Summer 1940

It's a Saturday, the second of September 1939 and Dad says I should remember this date because it's very important. He looked very serious when he told me he's almost certain we'll be at war with Germany in a day or two and lots of boys — and girls too, I suppose — are going to be evacuated. That means leaving home and going to the country. Before the end of the month I'll be eleven, so going on this bus — it's an Albion single-decker — to Denstone College will be an adventure, almost like going to a proper boarding school. Perhaps it'll be like Greyfriars School with Billy Bunter and Harry Wharton in *The Magnet* stories. And I can start my letters home with 'Dear Mater and Pater'. What a lark!

I think it's going to be exciting. Mum and Dad had big arguments about sending me away, but if Birmingham is going to be bombed by the Germans, then perhaps it's a good idea. Anyway, it's not going to be the first time I've been away from home. I've gone away lots, actually. I've stayed with Auntie Betty and Uncle Stan loads of times — and on the farm with their friends the Gleaves too — and with Dad's friend from work at the Bank, Uncle Eddie and his family. That's Auntie Linda and their daughters — Paula, who's a bit older than me and Mariane who's a bit younger.

Actually, I'm a bit sorry to be missing out on the bombing — I would probably be able to find bits of shrapnel for my collection. It's in my top drawer and Mum keeps complaining that it's untidy. In fact, it might be hard to find anything interesting, because Jerry wouldn't drop bombs near our house — not on purpose. It's just beside Highbury park, so it wouldn't be a target but it's not so very far from Cadbury's and the Austin, so there just might be a stray bomb somewhere close. Anyway, here I am, sitting about halfway down the bus with my gas mask in this stupid cardboard box on my lap. It's annoying because its sharp corners bang against my bare knees every time the bus hits a bump. I don't think there are more than two or three boys from my own school in Moseley, Woodroughs, coming along. Dad told me that I'm actually joining this other school from Edgbaston. It's The Edgbaston Preparatory School, or E.P.S., but they usually just call it Hallfield. They all seem friendly and their red and green caps are much better than mine. The Woodroughs cap is just a boring dull green all over.

Mum blubbed a bit when we said goodbye and I got on the bus at Hallfield. but loads of other mums did too, so I didn't feel too ashamed. Dad helped put my trunk on the roof, along with lots of others; Mine has a big yellow label with my name, Geoffrey Iley, written on it in large letters. More trunks, cases and boxes of bedding and stuff are in a lorry — it's a Morris Commercial, I think — and Mr. Rigby, the headmaster, said it would be following the bus. His own car, a Wolseley, is going to lead the way and another master, Mr. Fisher, will be at the back in his Austin.

The ride out of Birmingham was quite boring. just lots of houses, then some open country with cows and farms. After a while we went through a town with a funny name, Uttoxeter. We went past a big works called J. C. Bamford with lots of new farm machinery and tractors. It looked really interesting. Perhaps I can make machines and stuff like that one day. At last we went through a small village and up a hill and there was Denstone College. It's really big, with lots of grass and playing fields, but we were taken round the side to some rather old buildings that will be where we sleep and there are some classrooms too. I have got a bed in a big dormitory, but we have to go to the main school to have meals in their enormous dining room. Anyway, it's time for my first letter home — just a short note, as there's loads to do and some exploring too.

Saturday 2/9/39

Dear Mater & Pater

We had a lovely journey and arrived quite safely at 12.45. We are having a lovely time and have a very well lighted dorm which is roomy and airy.
The boys and masters are very nice. I am writing this card in the common-room. outside it is pouring. No more news.

Your loving son

Geoffrey

Now that's done, I can unpack my stuff. When the rain finally stops I'll have a proper look round. This is going to be very interesting.

* * *

After two days I've decided it's not good here after all, not like Greyfriars a bit. I'm really missing home for lots of reasons. For one thing there isn't any radio, so it came as a shock to hear that the war had actually started — I only heard about it the next day, on the fourth of September. There's nothing much to do here, either and I have had lots of tummyache. I think it's the awful food. The huge dining hall is horrible too. Us Hallfield boys have two tables at one end of this enormous room and the Denstone boys don't really speak to us. I really miss Mum's cooking. Honestly, I wish I was home again.

Tuesday 5/9/39

Dear Mater & Pater

Thank you very much for your letter. did you get my postcard? If you did put a chalk mark in your next letter, if not I will rub it off.
I am feeling terribly homesick and have tummy ache nearly every day because of the food. It is all undercooked.
I want to come home and will <u>walk</u> home* if a conveyance is not sent for me 5 days from now.

Your loving son,

Geoffrey

* and I mean that, Scout's honour I do.

That ought to do the trick, I think. But hang on a minute. Hello! I've just realised it's stopped raining and we're going to be allowed to go for a walk and look around a bit.

* * *

Actually the walk was good yesterday, and we can go again if we get permission first. There's some interesting exploring to be done around here and I've discovered we have a library with some jolly interesting books — I've found some about radio and one about marine engines. Perhaps it won't be too bad here after all, especially now that some of the boys have started to get parcels from home with food. Perhaps we'll be allowed to have tuck boxes, just like Greyfriars.

Monday 11/9/39

Thank you very much for the book. I have read one story already.

As regards a birthday present I would like a game of "Monte Carlo" (7s.6d.) or failing that a book on Heraldry, failing that a horse racing game called "Totopoly" (7s.6d.) failing that a loom from Lewis's (8s.11d.).

We have to have no more tuck sent or brought only apples & biscuits allowed.

P.S. Excuse the blot.

Great news! We're going to be allowed to start a Scout troop, so it was a good thing that I'd already joined at King's Heath back home. This will be fun. A lot of the boys are keen on sport, which I'm not much good at but the card games are good and we play rummy a lot. I like board games too — and chess.

Sunday 17/9/39

Thank you for the Chess set it arrived quite safely. We are forming a scout troop here with Vaughton, Herington, and I as patrol leaders. Please send uniform.

I enclose a tooth (back) which I pulled out on Saturday night and a dud "ever been had" £1 note.

Don't forget I'm looking forward to seeing you again.

P.S. Don't forget the birthday cake.

I know I only wrote yesterday, but it's really important they remember about the Scout stuff.

Monday 18/9/39

I hope you received my letter which I sent on Sunday. Don't forget to send my Scout uniform, also please send me an "Owl" patrol flag on a stave because as you know I am patrol leader of the "Owls". We are having four to a patrol. Yesterday Sandy Smith from our school (not Smith in Moor Green Lane) came.

It's my birthday today, but I'll write home anyway, I think.

Sunday 24/9/39

We went to a Holy Communion Service in the Chapel this morning, at which all the Denstone boys attended. the choir was one of the best I have ever heard.
The Robe of one of the ministers was the most magnificent of its kind I have ever seen it was made of Green velvet with a cross on the back in black rimmed with gold.
Have there been any raids on Birmingham yet?

Hooray! I did get a parcel on Monday. But Mr. Rigby was a bit shirty about some of the comics. It was good of Auntie Alice and Nana to send money for the 'Buccaneer' game. I will have to write and say thank you.

Sunday 1/10/39

Thank you for the Scout and other comics which arrived safely with letters. By the way Mr Rigby wants you to <u>stop</u> sending "<u>blood and thunders</u>" like the "Wizard", "Hotspur" & "Skipper" so please send me a suitable paper instead. Of course the "Scout" is quite all right. Thank you for the shoulder knot & Scout flag and "fag" cards they came about

Tuesday. The "owl" flag is very much admired. I regret to say that I am going to stop playing "Buccaneer" as the lid of the cylinder and one ruby have been lost, also the lid of the box has been bashed about.

We have now got nicely settled down to work and am getting used to the new books. Please tell Mr Rigby that I would like to take Greek and shooting if you can afford them.

Last night I learnt a new card trick from Mr England. We went to Chapel today and I never heard a choir sing so well.

Now I've got to write to Auntie Alice and Nana. I must remember to say thank you for sending the money for 'Buccaneer', but perhaps I won't say that it got a bit damaged.

Sunday 1/10/39

Dear Auntie & Nana,

Thank you very much for the money you sent. Mum bought a game of "Buccaneer" with it and I am getting a lot of fun out of it over here at Denstone. Oh! And thanks for the birthday cards you sent me.

Lots of Love

Geoffrey

We have started to do some shooting, which is great. I would like to shoot some Germans, but the war will be over before I get the chance. And I really would like to start music. I wonder what Mum and Dad will say.

Sunday 8/10/1939

Please can I take music here? If so please send my violin and bow & resin. m y violin & bow are in my cabinet & my resin is in either the top or bottom drawer of the bureau. I enclose my first target (shot with a B.S.A. air-gun). please send some bedroom slippers I need them badly. Thank you for the 'Scout' and the 'Boy's Own Paper'. Please send me some Geometrical instruments. Namely a pair of dividers a compass and a protractor (I think you can get them all at Woolworths Stationery Dept.) As well as writing to Nana I have written to aunty Edith and now I am going to write to a lot of other people. We have our places in form every three weeks when a <u>report</u> is sent to you. As regards the grey pullover I haven't seen a trace of it since I left home. Now its my turn to ask questions.

Are you all keeping well at home? Have you seen anything of the Dunbars lately? I wrote to them on my birthday but I haven't had any reply, The next time you write you will please tell me some war news? I want to know how things are getting on. Will you please send me a nice <u>long</u> letter next time you write or send anything.

<u>NEWS</u>

Every Sunday morning since we've been here we've had sosses every Sunday morning for brekker and its getting rather monotonous. Mind you I'm not complaining. On Friday it poured with rain but it cleared up, and as we were marching across for tea we saw a lovely rainbow. It lasted the longest I've known one to last.

On Wednesday we were examined by the Doctor. At first he could not make head or tail of me but after a bit he decided that I was all right. But first he declared that I & I of all people was flat footed.

The choir sang well today but the Bishop wore a new robe and when the choir came in, at the head of it were men with banners which is unusual.

I'm really starting to like it here and there are loads of things to do after lessons. For instance, I've started shooting with a .22 rifle.

We still don't get any news about the War — or only some time later. It's very annoying and worrying too. It seems a German U boat got into Scapa Flow and sank one of our biggest battleships. How could they do that?

I do miss news and seeing our neighbours at home, especially the Dunbars. I'm missing the fun I had making things with Ralph Dunbar in his Dad's workshop — and helping him mend his BSA motorbike. It would even be quite good to see his sister Kath, though she does get in the way sometimes. And she sings out of tune too. She's younger than me and she's always being a nuisance — a bit like my cousin Kathleen. That's the trouble with girls. Actually, I sort of miss her a bit, but her brother Derek even more. We had great fun every time we visited them in Ryhope. Auntie Alice used to get quite cross when Derek and I had our war games. That's because we were the gallant British and always made Kathleen be the horrible Germans. So, I'm feeling a bit blue. Still, mustn't let the parents know.

Sunday 15/10/39

Mr Fisher said that everything would be allright about the violin. please send it as soon as possible. I am <u>certain</u> that there is time I <u>want</u> to learn to play. It will not interfere with lessons at all.

I have just received a letter from the Dunbars with chocolate in it. Thanks for the parcel the geometrical instruments are superb. Thanks for the biscuits they are nice.

9

The rainbow was very colourful and it was just like a big archway over the hills. On Monday it absolutely poured with rain here. Did it at Birmingham? When I said that the doctor could not make head nor tail of me I meant that it took him a long time to make out whether I was alright or not. Yes the doctor did suggest a way to cure the flat footedness by foot exercises.

By the way I went to bed just after tea on Wednesday with dihorrea and got up on Saturday morning. on Saturday I saw the doctor again & he gave me some stuff (acid) out of a bottle marked "<u>poison</u>" strained it through some muslin and gave it to me to drink. Naturally I was rather hesitant about it but in the end I gulped it down. It <u>was</u> horrid it set my teeth on edge but I'm <u>not</u> dead yet by any means.

I have not yet asked anyone about the choir as it seems rather like swanking, as if I was saying "I think I'm good enough for the choir please let me in", so I haven't asked anyone yet.

The time of "Shooting" has been shifted to Monday. Last Monday it poured with rain so there wasn't any. In fact on Monday it was raining when we got up and did not stop for a second until after tea. As usual we had sosses for breakfast this morning. And we went to chapel this morning also as usual the choir sang very well. What I'm puzzled with is why have we had Holy Communion service five times running? I can't make it out there must be some freakish thing going on somewhere in the calendar. It's very mysterious. Oh! And its Harvest service I had quite forgotten for the moment. There were piles of carrots, parsnips, beetroot, cabbages, lettuces, spuds and things all over the place. There were the usual vestral garments this time and no banners or anything this week in fact it was rather dull after all the "stuff" last week.

Now for questions. Has Kath been in at all this week? Have

you heard any splutters from the motor bike lately? Are you all well? Any news of the war? Is it true about the Royal Oak? I can't think of anything more.

P.S. If it's too expensive I won't take music.

I quite like the work here and it's great to have so much to do and wonderful walks. But I really miss home and all the fun I had building dams in the stream. And the food keeps upsetting me.

Sunday 22.10.39

I hope you are well, as for myself I'm not. I was sick last night though I don't know what caused it. At the moment I'm feeling very groggy.

Thank you for the violin & case they arrived safely with resin and bow, and there was no damage done except that the bridge was broken right across. I'm going to get a new one from the music master here.

I enclose my first 22 target with proper ammunition. This is my first time shooting with a cartridge gun. I made a horrid mistake with the last target the real range was 7 yards.

NEWS

This morning I played a game invented by a boy called Herington my verdict is "very good". The game is rather like Buccaneer and is called "Pirate". Perrey's mother & father came on Wednesday and they said you might be coming today. They gave me some chocolate. I forget what day it was but sometime this week I passed my Tenderfoot test in the scouts, and got my Second Class card and so far in the Second Class I have passed two tests, compass & Kim's game.

Any news of the war? Have things started on a big scale on the western front? Seen the Dunbars?

P.S. Sorry but I had no time to write more.

After I sent this there was a letter from Mum saying there had been one or two bombs dropped in a raid on Birmingham, though nowhere near us and there wasn't much damage. so it seems the Germans aren't very serious. There doesn't seem to be anything happening in France either. I think the Germans will have to give up. They'll never get past the Maginot Line.

Mum and Dad keep asking questions about how I'm getting on. I really don't know what they worry about – perhaps I do lay it on a bit thick when I tell them that I've not been well. But I worry about them. Dad's really doing too much. He's putting in long hours at the bank because lots of the staff have been called up and he's an air raid warden too. And he's digging up part of the garden to grow vegetables. It's no wonder he passed out at the office.

Sunday 29/10/39

I'm quite all right now and back to lessons. I went back on Thursday. We went to Chapel this morning as usual. We had hymns unknown to me except for "Praise my Soul the King of Heaven" which I threw myself into and had a real good sing.

On Thursday Vaughton and myself went for a walk along the right of way that we saw on the right hand side of the road as we came back from the Railway Tavern. We came to a sort of River closed up at both ends, but the funny (peculiar) thing was, that the "River" was above ground level We made a hole in the bank and water trickled into the hollow but we got frightened as we thought it might cause a flood so we blocked the hole up quickly.

On Friday and Saturday we also went for walks and went and waded in the river. On Saturday we hid from the master (Dopey Russell) behind a haystack, and had a fine feed of blackberries. Yesterday a boy called Redmayne who sits next to me spilt a cup of tea all over himself at tea-time and had to do a lot of lines. Last supper time we had spaghetti (yum-yum), then sosses for breakfast this morning as usual and had mustard with mine. Two boys in our dormitory this morning made such a row they had to be reported to Mr Rigby. I've got a book out of the Library called "Scouting Games" and it is very interesting. Oh I forgot when we were coming back from the walk on Thursday we saw a very faint rainbow so we took its (and our) bearings so that we could have a look for the pot of gold the next time we went for a walk by ourselves (we could only see a bit of rainbow).

The other day Mr England tested me on Heraldry at a meal. I am quite warm in bed at nights thank you. of course the Second Class is much harder than the Tenderfoot. No I'm not going to read at night I never do. I will probably play some game or other. The apple was simply scrumptious and I bought some more from the fruit-man. I gave each of the boys in the sick room a slab. I asked the music teacher about the violin (*lessons*) and said that she would fix them up. Are your colds any better? I hope so. Is Dad perfectly all right after his fainting at the office? Have you seen anything unusual lately like a German bomber? Have many anti aircraft units gone past our house? Have there been any more air-raids? Have you seen the Dunbars lately? Any news from the Western front? What's Dad doing in A.R.P.?

P.S. Pardon my spelling of sosses.

Although it's Sunday, we're supposed to have inoculations today. I really hate them and hope I don't pass out or anything.

Sunday 5/11/39

I am going to be inoculated this morning by the Denstone school doctor. I hope I am having injections in the forearm

as it does not hurt so much there, whereas in the biceps it hurts like anything. I enclose a target (10 rounds, 30 yds) the reason why it is so bad is that the gun was too heavy for me. Last night we went to the Denstone Concert as a special treat. I'm wanted now for inoculation and I can't write any more.

Footnote from the headmaster: *Inoculation successfully done.* – *R.V.Rigby*

I'm quite excited because Mum and Dad are supposed to be coming on a visit at the week-end. We don't have a car, though Dad used to have one from the bank when we lived in Lincoln and he was an inspector, visiting branches all round the county. We haven't really needed one since. Of course, not many parents have cars, but Perrey says his Mum & Dad will give mine a lift. I can't wait to see them and have news from home.

Sunday 12/11/39

Thank you for your letters. I have not much time as I will be inoculated again soon. Are you coming today? Perrey says you are. If you have come, have you arrived home safely? How is everyone at home? How is the war going? How are the Dunbars? Has Kath been bothering you? Have you heard her "singing"? Have you heard the Dunbars motor bike spluttering any more? What has happened to the aeroplane I was making?

We've been told that instead of going home for the Christmas holiday, we are probably going to another place in the country. It will be in Wales, but it sounds to me as if it's going to be just like staying at school. Anyway, we have to ask our parents how they feel about it.

Sunday 19/11/39

For Christmas we are going away to some place in Wales pronounced (not spelt) Lannferfechan. We are going with several members of the staff, and Mr Rigby says that <u>you</u> <u>can</u> come and stay at the same boarding house or in the district for a week or so and some and see us as often as you like. We have been given our identity disks.

I have not yet written to grandpa though I may have time today.

I am not going to be inoculated today as I was done yesterday. As you say, I can now laugh at diphtheria germs. Can I go to that place in Wales?

How are you? In your next letter will you please tell me your birthdays again.

Please send me that game called "Invasion" for Christmas that you saw in the newsagents. Who is it made by? Waddingtons? Answer yes or no (Oh! No John no John no John no! *)

Please let me know as soon as poss if you can stay near me at Xmas.

* This does <u>not</u> mean that I do not want the game.

It seems like we really are going to Wales for Christmas. Actually it won't be too bad if Mum can come. Of course, Dad will have to stay behind because of the bank and I've just heard he might have to have an operation for a gastric ulcer, which worries me a lot. I'm sure he will be OK though, because he's always been quite fit.

I'm not quite sure how we're getting to Wales, but I think parents will join us later. If Mum could bring some of my stuff too, that would be super. It will be a shame to miss Christmas at home and seeing the Dunbars — and the Edwards' of course.

Paula and Mariane are great fun and they've taught me to play Pontoon.

Sunday 26/11/39

When you come to stay with me at Wales please bring me some ginger wine.

Please send my bike as soon as possible as the "extra" for Christmas and when you come do not forget to bring "Invasion" and with any postal orders you receive & please get my cinematograph fitted with a new adapter and bulb, and if poss get some films and bring the lot along when you come.

At shooting on Friday I shot 24 rounds on the target I usually send home and scored my first bull and had ten rounds on an "Imperial" target at thirty yards.

I am sleeping and keeping well thank-you and full of beans and bus-tickets. I had no time to write to Grandpa last time and I don't think I will have time this time. We went to chapel as usual today, and had sosses for breakfast.

Sorry about Dad. Will he have to have an operation? I hope not. As I write this I have a hole in my stocking about 6 sq. ins. in area. I'm not joking just stating fact. I have not seen about Dad's birthday yet so can you see about it? And I will pay you back when you come to Wales. My violin is coming on all right thank-you. Well we don't have weather here it rains all the time. They call me "mousey" here for some unknown reason and one boy gives me cheese (yum-yum). No more injections to come. we have a film show every Sunday, and did I enjoy the Denstone concert? I'll tell the world! I did not shoot last week as it was too wet. Have I tucked into the fruit? It's all gone. I am not having milk any more.

Every night it blows a Gale and in the last week or two, two lampshades have been smashed to smithereens in our dormitory alone, also the wind often wakes me up in the morning. How are you all at home? I hope you are keeping well. How is Kath? I have 8/- left (10/- less 2/- because of my watch being repaired) But can you buy a present for Mum and I will settle when you come for Christmas.

I must close now as I have no more time.

Mum wrote to say that Dad isn't going to need an operation after all, which is good news, though he has to have special food and some horrible medicine until he's better. We've had a bit more news about Wales. We will be at a seaside place, but I can't see the point, as it will be too cold in winter to swim or anything.

Sunday 3/12/39

Our exams begin tomorrow, and I am looking forward to them. About the bike. Mr. Rigby gave out a notice & stuck one on the notice-board saying that bikes <u>were definitely</u> allowed so please send mine. I think Mr Rigby said that there was enough room at the boarding house where we were going as only about 20 boys were going. I thought that we were going to Llanfairfechan not Borth. I could <u>not</u> write to Nana on Wednesday as we went for a 6¾ mile walk. On Friday we went for a much longer walk to a place called "Cromwells Battery". This was a hill, unclimbable on two sides and very rough ground on the other two. These rough slopes however were quite steep. We threw rocks over at one of the steep bits. The reason for calling the place "Cromwells Battery" was, that there was a manor beside the hill that was one of Cromwells strongholds, and the hill was used to mount the artillery defending the manor .

For Christmas could I have a new fuselage for my Frog Dive Bomber a new elevator & wings & some elastic (plenty of it) bring those together with the old machine to the boarding house with you please. *This is instead of the adaptor & bulb). When you come do <u>not</u> forget the Ginger Wine. I'm glad I had mumps before we went on holiday to Feltham. The boy who has mumps is called Sandilands.

Do you know how we are dealing with the magnetic mines? Please tell me in the next letter. Is there a set of laws about warfare? And if so are the Germans disobeying them? How can gargling and spraying help an abcess under a tooth? What do you mean "for drainage purposes"? How are you all? Any news of Kath? Have you heard any splutterings from Dunbar's motor bike?

Have you seen Ralph at all?

Mumps has started up at Denstone and we have got it too. I'm very glad to have had it already, so can't get it again.

Sunday 10/12/39

The epidemic of mumps is getting worse & worse. Yesterday Wheatley who sleeps next to me and Best caught it and already today Hackett & Gilbert have caught it. If it goes on at this rate there will not be any of the school left in 26 days. As I told you an aeroplane crashed 3 fields away it ran into a hedge & smashed the propeller and a wing. It was a Miles Magister Trainer. The boys were playing football when it flew over its engine kept cutting and then suddenly it swooped and we did not hear any more. Yesterday we played Smallwood Manor in pouring rain and we were soaked to the skin. We lost 4 – 0.

My bike has not come yet. At least if it has I have not seen it.

We went to the concert last night. there was an amusing Inspector Hornleigh play, then a conjuring trick. Then an "Albert" poem (you know the sort of thing, "A stick wit' 'orses 'edd 'andle the finest that Woolworths could sell"). Then a play of a rehearsal of Macbeth (very amusing). Then the surprise item a play acted by Leighton, Lawrence, Neales and Scarf. Called "The Rising o the Moon", that was just about the best as it was acted by Hallfield boys. It was about an escaped convict.

Mrs Rigby has given me my fruit. I will be able to bring my violin and Music. Do you know which warship of the Germans was hit? Oh! Don't forget the aeroplane, "Invasion", Ginger wine, cakes etc. and please buy all the required Christmas presents. All the exams are finished now, thank goodness and I have given you some results. Many happy returns whenever your birthday is in case I do not get a card in time to send it to you.

Any more war news?

After all the stuff about going to Wales, it seems as though everything's off and we are going home. It's because of the mumps, I think. Anyway I'm quite glad to be having Christmas at home. Then I can see everybody, hooray!

Christmas and New Year just flashed by and it's back to Hallfield in Edgbaston to get on the bus again. I still have my Woodrough's cap, though. Mum says I can have a Hallfield one at Easter.

Wednesday 17/1/40

Arrived safely but could not write yesterday before post went (3p.m.) Went on (organised) sliding expedition on ponds. One boy fell in.

E. P. S.
Denstone College
Uttoxeter
Staffs

Saturday 20/1/40

Dear Mr & Mrs Iley
Just a short note to let you know that all is well and Geoffrey seems to be enjoying life in this arctic condition which anyway will kill off any epidemic germs!
I note he will take Violin lessons and shooting as before.

With kindest regards,

Yours sincerely,

R V Rigby

It's really very cold here and all of us get badly chilled knees because of wearing shorts. and there's loads of snow but we haven't had a chance to go tobogganing yet.

Sunday 21/1/40

Thank you for the Scout but I have not had time to look at it yet. I enjoyed the sliding expedition very much thank-you. My cough is getting rather worse and my right side hurts when I cough. The present from Auntie Alice is a tin of sweets & a book called "The Hand & The Glove". It is a school story & is very interesting. We are frozen up here as well & it's perfectly horrible.
I say, have you heard the latest versions of "Whistle while you Work" they go like this and are distinctly anti-German.

Verse 1	Verse 2
"Whistle while you work	"Whistle while you work
Hitler is a twerp,	Musso bought a shirt,
Goering's barmy,	Hitler wore it,
So's his army,	Neville tore it,
Rub them in the dirt."	Whistle while you work."

We had an organised snowball fight yesterday and had lots of fun.

Actually, although I'm OK really, this cough is still pretty bad. It's still very cold too, but we are keeping reasonably warm when we are indoors.

Wednesday 24/1/40

I cannot go to the Doctor about my cough as Mr Rigby thinks I have a health phobia, and he would not take any notice and would not let me go, and my cough is getting worse & my capsules are running out.
P.S. This place is driving me barmy. Mr Rigby thinks that you have a health phobia as well.

Written on the back of the envelope

Don't write to Mr Rigby about this letter. Are you frozen badly?

It just keeps on snowing and snowing. I've just found out about censorship. when our troops write home, all their letters are censored and the censor puts a blue pencil through anything that shouldn't be mentioned. I'm going to try that on my next letter home. It should give Mum and Dad a laugh.

Tuesday 23/1/40

We have snow here 1ft 1in thick and one <u>small</u> drift about 1ft 6 ins thick. As you know the ponds are all frozen and the ice on them is about 10 ins thick but after this they will be thicker. It's as cold as *blue pencil* in the dormitory at night. When we go over to meals its always snowing and all the *blue pencil* snow goes down my *blue pencil* neck-hole. At night you often get off the path and wade into a *blue pencil* deep drift and the snow goes down my *blue pencil* wellingtons. I am doing *blue pencil* Greek now but in spite of the *blue pencil* I like it really. The other day I went sledging and went over a *blue pencil* precipice into a *blue pencil* hedge, and nearly broke my *blue pencil* neck. Are you still *blue pencil* well frozen up? We are. The oil and capsules arrived safely yesterday as well as the "Scout" & "B.O.P". Thanks. I hope Dad is all right now and going about just as *blue pencil* well as usual. (no offence meant by the *blue pencil*).

P.S. My *blue pencil* cough is getting better but my cold is rather worse.

<u>Censored by G. N. Iley</u>

Written on the back of the envelope

Please see if you can send me a chocolate cake (with icing). Don't forget to send more stamps.

The snow is getting even worse and we're having to help with lots of jobs to make sure we get supplies. Even the postman wasn't able to get through for a day or two.

Sunday 4/2/40

You will be pleased to know that I wrote to Auntie Alice & the Gleaves last Sunday and I am *blue pencil* well glad that they've written. I hear that you did not get my *blue pencil* letter until Friday. The reason is that the *blue pencil* letter-box was locked and the *blue pencil* postman could not get up here until Wednesday. I hear that you have a *blue pencil* food shortage in "Brum", so you may be wondering how we are getting on. As a matter of fact we are living on the <u>fat of the land</u>. the farmers cannot get rid of their milk and they give lots to us. (<u>As a matter of fact we have *blue pencil* got too much!</u>) We also bake our own bread so we are all right. as regards tuck I am *blue pencil* well all right except for fruit where I am running out. I got the parcel all right thanks.

Mr Rigby flatters me by what he says about me *blue pencil* well being a useful member of the community. For a pastime we have been lugging mail, meat and various provisions up and down on sledges. One Denstone master has skis they fascinate me it looks so easy. It has been pouring in the night and I hope it thaws, if it freezes we will be in a nice mess.

P.S. Why hasn't Dad written?

I actually got a letter from Dad during the week. It's good to know that he's feeling better now.

Sunday 11/2/40

I am glad to say that my *blue pencil* cold & cough are much better now. Perrey says that you are coming today with his parents. The next time I go to music I will ask about a violin. You asked me about new members of staff in a letter last week. The new members are: - Miss Mathews (see P.S.)

in place of Miss Hostle, and a Mr Woodfine in place of Mr England who has joined up. Mr Woodfine is nicknamed "Fag End" because a boy here on first hearing his name though that it was Mr. "Woodbine".

A lot of us here have maps of non-existent islands of which we imagine ourselves possessors. We nab bits of paper and old exercise books with a few clean pages for notes of wars (we are always having wars) against non-existent countries. I am no exception to the rule and have not an island but a portion of mainland. It is called "Subitar" and has already grabbed quite a few colonies. Can I join in the "Lend to Defend" scheme? If so send along my post office book and it can be exchanged for the right amount of certificates. You can cash the certificates when you like just like the post office and you get more interest.

P.S. Miss Mathews has been replaced by a Miss Deerdon.

It is still very cold and the wind is biting too. We envy the Denstone boys with their long trousers.

1. Bare knees in the snow

Sunday 18/2/40

I pulled out two teeth yesterday. It has been snowing here again and everything is snowed up, and we had a terrible job to get over from the san. With the money that you sent I bought 4 savings certificates and twelve 6d stamps to put in a special book. The report here shows that I have gained one place in VI. We had a snowball fight yesterday and I got soaking wet. We went to the pictures on Wednesday & saw "Jew Süss". My Heston Phoenix has not arrived yet. I have no time to write more.
P.S. Ward Ma. and I will go bird nesting when the eggs are in. Please see if you can send an egg-blower and a partitioned box (fairly big).

I'm really getting into aeromodelling, but there are loads of other things to do. Actually, it's only because we're indoors so much because of the horrible weather. I can't wait for it to get a bit warmer so that we an go exploring and find out where are good places to look for bird's eggs.

Sunday 25/2/40

Subitar (see P.S.) is getting on very well & I have made £325,000 since I last wrote by selling some plans of an aeroplane namely "The Kara fighter or light bomber" together with 25 of its kind.
It has:- 1 shell gun in propellor boss
4 machine guns in each wing
2 in a turret
The planes cost £12,000 each
The plans cost £25,000
How are you both? I hope you are much better. When I asked for a box please see if you can get a proper birds egg

case & don't forget the blower. A German measles epidemic has started here & a lot of Denstone boys have got it as well as us. I cannot get on with the aeroplane as you have not sent the blue prints for it. The tail was broken in transport but I think I can mend it. I have finished the book that you sent & I enjoyed it very much. Please see if you can send me a 6d penguin book (murder story). The cake was very nice thank you it was enjoyed by all. Mr Fisher has just given me this weeks stamps. Please send me some more fruit I am running out. My glove fell in the river the other day and got lost. We went for a cross country run in the snow the other day. No more news.

P.S. Subitar in case you forgot is my country.

P.P.S. Please send some more stamps.

I was glad to get Mum's letter along with a parcel and to hear that she's better now. and Dad too. I expect it's the better weather. They're trying to persuade us to go to Wales again in the holiday. I really don't want to go.

Sunday 3/3/40

I think that the Spring is really coming. Thank you very much for the parcel it arrived safely on Saturday. Miss Maclure says that she needs a written request from you about the violin. We went to a play last night and I cannot enclose the programme as Mrs Rigby took my wallet as my pocket was bulging. I can't help it as I have nowhere else to put the wallet.

The term ends on the 20/3/40 and a bus will be sent to take us back to Birmingham.

There will be a holiday party at Llanfairfechan but I would like to come home instead (the Llanfairfechan party is not compulsory).

<u>"Indignation"</u> I think that we should come home as:-

(a) All the rest of the Birmingham schools are back except ours. (This information was gained from Mr Painter)
(b) I, II, III are going back permanently but not* IV, V, VI. (From Mr Painter)
(c) Brum is almost impregnable to air attack.

*raspberries

Hooray! The Llanfairfechan trip is not going to happen. That's very good news.

Sunday 17/3/40

You will be pleased to know (I don't think) that I have had German measles. I was in bed from Monday to Thursday morning. I am now quite O.K. but my cough and cold are troubling me a lot and when I come back home I intend to stay in bed till I am better.

There was a shooting competition on Saturday and I was third getting a score of 49. Actually I got 43 (record) but I had a handicap of 6 making 49, 2nd got 50, 1st got 51.

Well, I will soon be home now and there are many pleasant signs of this the most obvious is all the trunks being out in the dorm. But if you go along at night you nearly break your neck. When we go back next term I will be 4th in the school and possibly a prefect.

When I come home I shall arrive at about 12.30 on the bus. Mr Rigby will not allow my bike to be sent home.

I am in the finals of the Elocution as a reserve; but I do not think I will be called upon to say my piece.

P.S. We went to the Palm Sunday service and all got little palm leaf crosses.

The Easter holiday seems to be flashing past. I've spent a lot of time at the Edwards', playing pontoon and gin rummy with Paula and Mariane. I went round to the Dunbars once or twice too and Ralph has got very keen on "Invasion". It's a nuisance that the skin trouble I had when I was little seems to have come back, but it's not much to worry about – not yet anyway.

Postcard — Tuesday 30/4/40

Arrived safely had nice lunch. Am now playing "Invasion" with Smith, Dawe & Homer. I have got 5 army corps.

It's so much better back at Denstone this term. the weather's better and we have a better dorm too.

Sunday 5/5/40

Glad to receive your letters and the Scout. Please just send two letters a week one in the "Scout" & the other on Monday. "Invasion" is very popular and is becoming a craze. You will be pleased to hear that my nails are still intact. Lessons are going O.K. & I am doing much better at "Caesar".
We are now sleeping in the old playroom and are not using the san annexe for any purpose at all. The Denstone boys are now back.
We had our first cricket game yesterday and I made 3 before being got out by a fast one that went between my bat and my legs. We are now getting settled down to work and I am doing rather better than last term. I am now turning into a demon fast bowler (better than at home) & am practicing hard (they are mostly on the wicket & I don't have many wides). I hope this does not sound like boasting but it's a fact.

Music and Shooting have not started yet; but as I have told you we are settling down nicely. I hope you are both well. I have got no contracts for plans yet but Smith ma. will probably buy some "CELBA" C.5 Flying Boats.

Subitar is doing very well against our deadly enemies the Quisticanians, who are losing ground to us in Flestaria. I hope that Mum and Dad are following all this. Perhaps I could be a general one day.

Wednesday 19/5/40

Thanks for your letter & the parcel. They arrived safely on Friday. We played golf last night & had quite a good game but one ball lost. Hinde & I are attacking Flestaria, a Quisticanian Colony with great success. The Ryvita is going down well & I have finished the brown loaf. We are nicely settled down again & are getting used to work. I have not finished the "Public School Murder" yet but I have read "The War of the Worlds" by H G Wells. It's a jolly good book & it is about some Martians who came to the Earth because Mars was getting too cold for them to live on. When they came they tried to conquer the world with a heat ray & poison gas (this was before aeroplanes or gas masks) but they all got killed off by disease which does not exist in Mars but before they were killed they built a flying machine from which we got the aeroplane. But all attempts to analyse the heat ray & poison gas failed. And it was suspected that they were an unanalysed band of the spectrum.

Mum sent some special cream for me to rub on the place where my skin is flaking, so I hope it will do the trick.

Sunday 26/5/40

Thank you for the Scout and the B.O.P. the Psoriasis is getting on alright now. My knees & elbows have stopped but my feet & heels have started peeling. Please send me some more lime juice & brown bread as I am running out. My sweets are getting low but I think I can manage till the end of the week ending June 2nd. We had air-raid practice on Wednesday and missed part of a Latin Lesson. Have you received my report yet? I hope you are satisfied being as I am still in same position as at beginning of term. Please note 100 conduct marks. Please send report back as soon as possible.

We are now writing letters before we go to chapel and last week it was simply marvellous with lots of banners & candle bearers etc. Please will you tell me when you are coming next, as Wheatley has offered to take me out next Sunday if you are not coming. <u>Please send me some news about the Political situation we scarcely know anything here except that the Germans (blue-pencil them) are in France.</u> I have had my first violin lesson from a man called Mr Gibson. He accompanies me on the <u>violin</u>!

I can't find out much about what the Germans are up to. I suppose we should be worried but I'm sure our lads are a match for them any day.

Saturday 2/6/40

My skin is getting on alright but the palms of my hands have started peeling. I feel very well indeed except for a cold & my eyes going funny (peculiar). I have just stuck stamps in my savings book to the value of 5/- for the 5 Sundays we have been here.

The VI form challenged the rest of the school. We won the rest made 63 & we made 105 of which I made 7 before being caught off a fast spinner that glanced off the edge of my bat. My runs average is now 41/6 which is very low, but the reason is because I am a stonewaller. Its a very hot day here & the Denstone boys are clearing out the swimming pool & I wish I had my swimming costume. You know that Spitfire I started to make at home well don't throw it away because I have an idea so that I can make it so that it will fly. I am making a little aeroplane (glider) out of paper & scrap balsa & it looks quite good. Please send me a very cheap kit sometime. We had gas-mask drill on Monday. No more news.

It's so very hot! Nobody wants to go out much as it's cooler to stay indoors and read or play cards or "Invasion".

Sunday 9/6/40

We are being roasted out here and if it wasn't for the swimming pool, I expect I would be a shrivelled-up corpse by now. We had bathing every day except for Saturday when we played cricket & was I hot? Or was I hot?? (I'll tell the world!!!) I am going out with Wheatley today probably. I expect Dad is looking tired & washed out these days being out till <u>2a.m</u>. I like the sandals and they are very comfortable. Every time I bathe get a pain in the head at the back and I don't know what causes it. I am reading "Know Ye Not Agincourt" from the Denstone library "Round the Moon" from the Hallfield library and a book called the "Vintage Murder". Please send me a box of leads as I have found an unclaimed propelling pencil. Please see if you can do anything about a tennis racket as I played last night and liked it and please get me one about 11½ oz. My psoriasis is rather better now.

Sunday 16.6.40

I have been beginning to find out the joys of swimming. I scarcely need to move my arms and legs at all to keep afloat. I am managing to float a little bit now and am a deep-ender. I am wearing longs today for chapel as my other suit is being cleaned. We played cricket yesterday & I did not get an innings as we were declared at 103 for 3 wickets. My average is now 51/3 & the last time I played I got 7 not out.

I have heard that Paris has been taken & that Turkey is on the verge of war. We have also heard that Italy is in & we have captured 2 Libyan forts & one of our cruisers has been sunk.

It has been lovely weather lately but today the skies are overcast. Let us hope that since the Germans were winning on fine days it means that we will gain a victory on clouded ones. I hope the French Foreign Legion & the Spahis are doing well on their front in Libya. The psoriasis is getting better & my hands have stopped peeling. Don't forget to send the Kit. I hope you are both well.

We have finally started to get some news. It's not very good and some of the boys are a bit worried. Auntie Betty and Nana are staying at our house for a bit, but I'm not sure if they'll still be there when I go home for the summer holiday.

Sunday 23/6/40

Thank you for the parcel & especially the fudge & tomato juice but as Mrs Rigby has perhaps told you of the aeroplane kit, there is no trace. I hope you will come on the week-end (Saturday included) as there is a Red cross fête with side-shows being held at Denstone & on the Sunday there is a fathers' match being held here on the Saturday. Tea is provided at both but you will have to bring a picnic tea. (Official communiqué). The psoriasis has almost entirely disappeared except for a peeling between the toes. The Wheatley's took me out as you may have heard from them. In case I did not tell you Nana wrote the other week. I am glad to hear that she and Auntie Betty are staying at our house for a few weeks. I am very sorry to hear about Auntie Betty & Uncle Stan having to move it will be very hard on them. We heard the other day that the Italian air defences in N. Italy were so bad that some of the A.A. Gunners were shot by the Italian authorities the next time we made a raid the A.A. Gunners were so keen they shot down 8 of their own machines. We have also heard another heartening piece of news, that an Italian destroyer was captured by one of our trawlers. we ought to send lots of trawlers to the Italian coast to capture their navy.

Lots of love to you, Nana & Auntie Betty

It's good to know that Mum and Dad can come next week end, but as they will be having a lift from the Perry's, they may not be able to stay for all of the fête.

Sunday 30/6/40

This is going to be a short letter. I spent the 2/- on shove-ha'penny. Mr Woodfine started another stall after you left. I was in charge of a hoop-la stall and took 25/- in ½ hour. I have stuck the elevator on the aeroplane & have finished one wing & started another. There were no air raids last night.

I was a bit surprised to have a letter from Dad, he doesn't often have time to write. What he said was very surprising and worrying too. It was brilliant that we got so many of our people away from Dunkirk, but loads of tanks and artillery had to be left behind. I think Mum and dad want to get me out of the country. They seem to think it's a good idea for me to go to America or Canada in case the Germans invade. That just can't happen can it?

Saturday 6/7/40

I considered Dad's letter very carefully & have found that the favours lie in going, i.e.

For Going	Against Going
1. Good of Country	1. A big hole in your pocket
2. Your freedom from worry	2. Homesickness
3. My own safety	3. I am there for duration
4. My educational interest	4. It is impossible for you to see me
5. My general & personal interest	
6. Health etc.	

Therefore all points lie in favour of going. Therefore although it is hard to do so I will go.
When I go I would rather go to the U.S.A. if you don't mind. I have now completely finished my aeroplane complete with camouflage. I tried to fly it once but the wind was too strong so I brought it in. I will send it up to Hallfield with Mrs Rigby as soon as possible. We are having a fete of our own (unofficial) today & I am in charge of a stall in which you are blindfolded and you attempt to pin Hitler's moustache on in

the right place. Nearest of the day wins 10 sweet prize. Weather has been fine except for the heavy shower that you mentioned in your letter.

I put some light-hearted stuff in my last letter, but this business about leaving for another country is still very hard to think about. I need a bit more information.

Sunday 14/7/40

There are quite a few things I forgot to ask you about in my last weeks letter.

(i)   When, if you can tell me anything about it, I am going 'cross the Atlantic? (see) P.S.
(ii) Will any of you accompany me on the journey.
(iii) To What part of the Continent I am going. (From what you said I prefer Canada).
(iv) To which state if poss.
(v)   To which town I am going.

Please can you tell me whether I could come to Hallfield by bus (official) for the sports. (July 20th)
But if there are not enough boys going sports of our own will be held on the 27th. There will be camping in the holidays but I would rather come home instead of camping so that I can see you before I go.
About the unofficial fete I made a profit on my stall of 6 sweets and won another 6 at a table owned by another boy.
I sent home my aeroplane via Mrs Rigby on Friday and I think it is at Hallfield at the Moment. We had a lovely walk last Sunday and kept on ambushing Mr Fisher & chasing him. We are practicing for the Sports now.
P.S. I hope I don't get torpedoed or Marri-ed to a Merma-id

at the bottom of the deep blue sea.

Well the sports went well, but I didn't win anything. Mum and Dad came and brought Nana along too. Didn't mind going back to Denstone really, as it's almost the end of term and I shan't be going to any camp, so that's all right.

Postcard — Saturday 20/7/40

Arrived safely. Just discovered that I have Nana's pen here. Played "Scats" with Hinde & Won.

I suppose I ought to have sent a bit more than a postcard, so I'll send a letter too, even though there's no news since yesterday.

Sunday 21/7/40

This is going to be a waste of paper & 2½d as I can't think of anything to say. Well, we arrived back at about 10.15 and were in bed about 10.20. The journey seemed to go very quickly. I enjoyed the sandwiches and gave the soss rolls to Hinde. We got up at 8.20 after I had read a lot of a thriller. I had some milk, a soss and a piece of brown bread and Marmite. then I came to write my letter, and that's all there is to say.
P.S. Don't forget to look after the aeroplane and the elevator Nana put in her bag.

Well, it's back home for the summer holiday. I gave Nana her pen back and she gave me half a crown, which was jolly decent of her. She really isn't bad even though she's so old. Glad to say that the idea of sending me away to the other side of the Atlantic seems to have faded a bit. I hope it disappears altogether.

We went to Llandudno on the train for a holiday.

2. Mum and Dad on holiday at Llandudno

We stayed in a big hotel and went to see a funny play at the theatre on the pier. I had a great time in the shooting galleries too.

But we soon had to come home again and I had to think about going back to Denstone.

Year Two

Autumn 1940 — Summer 1941

Sunday 22/9/40

We had a lovely journey. We saw the Messerschmitt fighter which was brought down, at the Hall of Memory. It had a yellow nose, and apart from the fact that the propellor was bent up no damage appeared to have been done to it at all. On the way to Lichfield we passed a long column of troops, some of which were Canadian, in full fighting kit. We started lessons on Friday. Everything has arrived here except my health certificate and ration card. If you look in the drawers of the tantalus you will find some conkers please send them with the birthday gear. We had quite a good nights rest, but we heard a plane, then the warning at Uttoxeter and the all clear at the same place later on. You need not bother to send my bike at all I don't really want it. We had a hail-storm here which lasted about 5 to 10 minutes on Thursday. Don't forget to send the envelopes.

This has been a rather boring week.

Monday 7/10/40

I can't think of much to say today, but all the same "A man might try". Oh! But haven't I? We had a pitched battle with some Denstone boys yesterday, using acorns to throw at them.
We could not finish the battle as we had to go in for prep but the result on the whole was indecisive. Luckily the authorities do not know about it, or we would be well and

truly in the soup. Are you sending me some hair-oil? If not please do as soon as poss as my hair is getting in a mess. Thanks for sending the aeroplane when it comes.

The Germans have started more air raids and Dad's said they are building air raid shelters in the gardens of houses in Shutlock Lane.

Saturday 12/10/40

Thank you very much for the tuck, kit etc.
Please tell me what position I came out in the quarterly. Was the "newsy" in the last letter meant to be sarcastic? The Aeromodeller arrived O.K. thank you. Is the air raid shelter finished yet? How many bunks are there? Is it crowded with the props in it? We are having lots of warnings here but we don't get up or anything for them, but I think I saw a Jerry Plane. It had square wing tips but was not painted yellow like the "Magister" trainer which I think is the only square tipped plane in the British air force. If it was a Jerry it was probably a Messerschmitt 109.
I only got money for presents. This is my record I think for money at a birthday 28/-. We did not have a beano when Hinde had his birthday.
I was sick yesterday and had to stay in bed all day. Once I went terribly weak in the afternoon as I had had no food or drink since the last suppertime. I was in the lavatory at the time and I staggered out terribly dizzily with mist before my eyes and had just enough strength to get back to my bed. but I am all right now.

I am absolutely OK now. It was obviously some tummy bug. Just got a long letter from Mum. Auntie Betty and Uncle Stan have come over to collect Nana. they have a lovely little smooth haired terrier and I wish I could see her.

Postcard — Sunday 13/10/40

Thank you for the long letter I received on Tuesday. Jane is a nice dog isn't she? How does she like air-raids? Where does she sleep? Please send some balsa cement on Saturday with your letter. (There is some in the box of my other plane).

I'm getting on like a house on fire with my aeromodelling.

Sunday 27/10/40

The weather has not been very warm this week. When we played at Abbotsholme we won 3-0. I was XII man and played linesman. We had cycled over and I borrowed someone's bike it was lovely. It was scarcely any effort at all to ride compared with mine as it had a three speed and also was a light bike. They gave us a lovely tea compared with Denstone with cakes and was almost like "holme*" (please laugh here). There was a crazy match yesterday and everyone played the position he was worst at. I played centre-forward and had the luck to score one goal. Our side won 1-0.
My plane is almost finished now except for fitting prop and noseblock and I have not covered it or made the undercarriage. Do not bother to send the cutter as I don't think I will need it any more. I have done a sudden going up of marks in Arith and Latin (please don't think I'm swanking) but in Arith the other day I got 16/18 and in Latin 27/30. Please send me Uncle Tom and Auntie Kittie's address.

It seems quite a long time ago now since my birthday. I really must get on with the rest of my thank you letters. One of my presents was a conjuring set and I'm getting quite a whiz at some of the tricks.

Sunday 10/11/40

It has rained yesterday and is raining today. I have mastered the card locator quite well thank-you. With the remaining 6d I have purchased a "dinkie-toy" and am very satisfied with the bargain. Under my fort, which is in my wardrobe you will find together with my soldiers some cars one is a mechanical horse and trailer and a yellow and orange racing car. If there is another "dinkie-toy" you will find this stamped on the underside of the car please send it with the other vehicles. Please purchase out of my money a good amount of plasticene to weight the car. Also please take 2/6 of my money and buy some "dinkie-toys".

On Saturday and Thursday in the dormitory we held plays in both of which I took part. In the latter I was Chief Inspector Stanley C.I.D. and shot Hinde, a member of the "Blue Diamond" gang. In the former I was Hans Bolthstein a German spy. I again shot Hinde but only badly wounded him I also shot Longland in the hand but was later on shot fatally by Hinde. I also played the part of a German messenger, Steiner who came to collect stolen plans. I again got shot. I spoke (please don't think I am swanking) with a beautiful German accent and everyone said that I played the part very well.

The parcel arrived back safely and Miss Taylor got the chocolates. She is going to write back and thank you. Mr Rigby has got my report.

P.S. Please send some more tuck.

The violin is going quite well, but I don't like practicing much.

What I like best at the moment is trying to think of ideas for plays.

Sunday 17/11/40

It is raining hard today and has been ever since I woke up this morning. I have written a play called "X.33 at Bay" which is a plot to blow up the battleship "Invicta". I play X.33 foiled and eventually shot by Hinde as S.27 of the British secret service.
I played football the day before yesterday, played centre-forward and scored one goal. I hope the dinkie-toys will arrive safely thankyou for the 4d extra. A rat has nibbled a hole in the lining and pocket of my mack. I don't know about being a Kreisler but I would like to learn to play every musical instrument I could lay my hands on. There have not been any more recitals at least we haven't heard of or been to any. We went past Stabwood on a walk with Mr Rigby the other day.

I think I'm getting more used to the food, though we do seem to get hungry. but Mum still seems to be able to get enough ingredients to send a cake from home sometimes, and she wants to know what I would like for Christmas, which isn't too far away now.

Sunday 24/11/40

Thank you very much for the dinkie-toys and the etceteras. I did not expect a cake. Thank you very much for it. Thank you very much for your generous offer I would like very much to join the Childrens' book club for 1 year. I enclose the form. Thank you very much for the plans of the shelter. Please can I have for the plane either (Choose yourself - I

43

enclose prices). the M.S. "Sportster (6/2) made by "Keelbild" not to be confused with "Kielkraft" or the M.S. "Dragonfly" (5/6) by "Keelbild" or the "airacobra (6/6) by "Atlanta" or a "Hawker Hurricane" (3/3) by "Tower" or the "Caudron Renault Racer" (3/3) by "Northern Model Aircraft Co.

We shot against Smallwood in a competition on Wednesday we lost, they got 544 and we 515 out of a possible 600. Their top boy got 98 out of a possible 100. I was second on our team our first boy getting 93 and I got 92.

N.B. We have got a whooping cough epidemic here.

The whooping cough is quite bad, but I had it when I was much younger, so can't catch it again. There have been more raids on Birmingham, Mum & Dad say there's been nothing much nothing near our part of the city. News about the war is still very hard to get here.

Sunday 1/12/40

Thank you for the letter which arrived on Thursday. Please do not buy me a plane for Christmas and could I have a wireless licence in the New Year instead unless you allow me to buy one with postal orders. Please can I take up wireless telegraphy as I have found a book which is a real gold mine of circuits signs, etc. There is a boy here by name Barker who is also keen and has a five-valver of his own construction at home. He is under contract in the holidays to build me a one-valve set for 2/- (without batteries or earphones. The earphones can be substituted by my loud-speaker.

Since my last football report I have scored 5 goals.

Have you had any more bad raids yet? The other night we heard waves and waves of aeroplanes going over. Has the "Aeromodeller" come in yet? Please send it as soon as

possible. Please tell me what the Greeks are doing and how far they are from Durazzo. What is happening to the huge mass of Italian troops that have just been rushed up?
P.S. We heard 2 terrific crashes on Friday night.

The parents are thinking that I shouldn't come home for Christmas because of the air raids, but I think that's stupid.

Sunday 8/12/40

Just think in a week I will come home for Christmas. that is if you will let me. Can't I come home for Christmas? I have more school than holiday without staying for Christmas??!!!! It's Preposterous!! Unbelievable!! And you just wrote home and said that you had not had a raid for 3 days!!! Why stay at Denstone?? At my birthday Auntie Betty wrote saying "could I come over for Xmas?" If things got bad you could easily pack me up to Walpole. Have you had the Aeromodeller yet? Have you considered the wireless? This term seems to have gone terribly quickly. I have scored one goal since last report.
P.S. We have not been inoculated for Typhoid. Is there an epidemic at Brum?

Dad's now Head Warden and gets a white helmet instead of a black one. Crikey, I've forgotten about his birthday and it's Mum's too in another few days.

Postcard — Monday 9/12/40

Many happy returns of both your birthdays when they come. When I realized that I had forgotten to write enclosing birthday wishes I was very ashamed so here we are. You need not bother with the plane as there are

batteries etc., to buy which are rather dear. Could you please get a 120 volt battery instead of it. I am pleased to hear about the licence. I am wearing my grey flannel suit (shorts). My shoes are still watertight. So here's till the holidays.
P.S. Congratulations to Dad for being promoted (ARP).

Well, it could be a lot worse. Just a few of us — Walker, Bill Harrison and his sister Jill — are staying at a lovely old house near Hereford, well away from Birmingham. Mum will be here for part of the time, so Christmas won't be so bad. Miss Taylor will be here all the time, I think. She is very jolly and a really good sport. Her artificial leg doesn't seem to bother her at all. She told us that when she was little she was run over by a tram, which sounds horrible.

Whitwick Manor

Wednesday 10/01/40

Thank you for the letter. I am coming home next Sunday according to Miss Taylor who has been rung up by Mr Rigby to say so. Walker's parents are coming on Monday to take him home and Jill is going on Wednesday. We went for a walk the other day and saw a dead badger. We went to Cowan Court some days ago and explored it but we can't find any way into the cellars.
We saw a rabbit yesterday, we had a bow and arrow but no time to fire so he got away. I have read the Prize Budget for Boys. I enclose a letter sent to you but as I did not go down to Newtown I could not re-direct it. Hope you are well. No more news.
P.S. I have had a letter from Barker about the Wireless we are going to make next term. Miss Taylor sends her "most passionate and loving remembrances" (to put it in Miss

Taylor's own words)
P.P.S. Mr Bray has got pleurisy. At Miss Taylor's suggestion
we are going to form a band as follows:
<u>Tinleg Watarowskis Super Orchestra</u>
Tinleg Watarowski (Miss Taylor) Piano
Ivor Nastikoff (Me) Violin
Ursinia Popoffski (Jill) Mouth Organ
Maestro Canniplayski (Bill) Comb & Tissue Paper

The good news is that the term is starting late because
Hallfield is moving! Mr. Rigby really wanted us to be in a place
of our own, so that we wouldn't be lodgers at Denstone. but it's
taken a while to find somewhere and get it all fixed up, so we
will get a few more days holiday.

E.P.S.Hallfield
Sidway
Nr Market Drayton
Salop

Sunday 26/1/41

Above is the correct postal address. Sidway is a lovely old-
fashioned house built in 1896. Our dorm. is very old indeed,
the oak panelling having been brought from an old manor.
The fireplace and cupboard are hand carved. We have a <u>coal
fire</u> in the dorm at night. We have actually had a billiard
table fixed up; it is very big about 8' x 4'.
In the bus I used the <u>sneezing powder</u> and did it work or
did it work? It nearly blew everyone up. We arrived at about
4.15 after a long journey. We had dinner at 4.30 (soss &
mash). We played billiards on Friday for the first time in the
evening. My record break so far is 9.
In break on Friday when we started school we went for a

walk. Hinde, Longland, Walker & Myself were versus the rest in a snowball fight but we were overpowered by weight of numbers. In the afternoon we went and manhandled wood from the wood (about 100 yards away) to the house for firewood. On Saturday we went for a walk through some woods. We snowballed Walker who got into a temper and flew at Ward. Darling pounced on him and overpowered him but he broke away and ran back to Sidway. There has been no row (as yet).

Although we've had loads of snow, it isn't as cold as it was at Denstone. That's because we have lovely fires. Anyway, the snow is starting to melt now.

Sunday 2/2/41

Thank you for the letter. We have a coal fire every night and it is sometimes possible to see the wall at the other end quite clearly. We have reasons for ragging Walker. (a) He grumbles like anything. (b) He is a cad. (c) He is a nuisance. (d) He asks unnecessary questions.

I have Capsules regularly and am having my fruit. My winter underwear has not yet been unearthed. I did not get scragged for the sneezing powder because no-one found out not even Miss Taylor and Hinde & Longland helped to blow it.

I have not yet done any practicing. The food here is almost as good as I get at home. And we have lovely Shepherd's pies. About if I want anything sent; I would be very pleased if you could go to the wireless shop (it's almost next door to the Kings Heath library) and get:- a tuning condenser (triple; second hand) and a valve (second hand) at about 1/6 and not from that shop a 120 volt or over battery (about 7/6). Barker has come and we have started the wireless it is now complete except for a battery and valve. We can fix up an aerial and earth here. The mike works well (and how!). We went for a 7 mile walk yesterday and were we tired or were we tired?!! We went to Maer church today and the choir sang all out of tune on the high parts of one of the hymns. I only knew one hymn they sang. ("The God of Love my Shepherd is")

This place is so much better than Denstone. and there are some much more interesting walks. We have started to do plays here and Smith likes writing them too.

Sunday 16/2/41

Thanks for the Aeromodeller. I have finished 'Oxus in Summer', it was a very good book. As we started late, this term will be extended to April 9th.
We have done some rabbit-snaring but no-one has caught a rabbit yet. We have also set about 3 bird traps. It has a sort of platform to put bread or corn on and a noose. It is impossible to describe how it works without seeing the trap, but when the bird walks on the platform to get the food, it gets caught by the noose.
On Wednesday we had shooting but I did not do very well as the gun was rather heavy. We went to church this morning by car and walked back. Mr Rigby did about 50 M.P.H. all the way. I enclose my report. Hinde got 384 Smith got 359 and I got 346, so we were pretty close.
We have had a play in which I was Steinmund a Gestapo official who, finding things too hot for him in Germany goes to England as a spy. It was the play that I wrote last term joined on to one of Smith's. We played football yesterday but it was very tiring and hot. We are doing Ovid and Livy this term. We are going to do a command perfor-

mance of the play this afternoon or tonight. I am going to start the Jacob's book soon. I am wearing my winter underwear today. It is drizzling this afternoon so I won't go out. Please send my stamp album and a wallet full of stamps if you can find it (I think it is in my top dressing table drawer).

P.S. I wrote to Paula <u>last</u> Sunday. Please send some more envelopes.

Mum and Dad are starting to think about my next school, because I will have to go to a different one in September, when I shall have my thirteenth birthday. Mr. Rigby has a plan to enter Smith, Hinde and me for the King Edwards exams to see what our standard is like.

Sunday 23/2/41

I received the parcel safely yesterday. Thank you for the Weetabix and honey. But it is not much good sending cereals as we are not allowed to eat them. We are taking exams on March the 12th and 13th. Even if I do pass have I got to go to King Edwards? I do so want to go to Malvern with Hinde (I think I could get a £100 scholarship) at the same time he does because we probably would be able to share a study.

There will be a parents weekend on Sat. March 15 and Sun. March 16. We can go out on Saturday from 5 – 6.30 p.m. If you want to stay the night, the nearest Hotel where accommodation is to be had is 10 miles away. the "Castle" at Newcastle. There will be one inter-team match on Saturday March 13. There will be tea at 4 p.m. for parents on Saturday and possibly on Sunday. We will be able to go out on Sunday from 12 – 6.

We have lots of snow here and had a lovely snowball fight. It was a running fight but we cornered the enemy so they surrendered. I have had a violin case bought for me and some resin. On Wednesday we had shooting. I got 13 this time on a five bull target. We don't get any warnings here. I have just found that I have got an uncatalogued stamp. It is from Burma. We are going to have another play next Sunday. It condemns "Careless Talk".

Mum and Dad came over for the week end. they wanted to see Sidway (and me!) but also to talk to Mr Rigby about exams and schools. The idea is to go for the King Edwards scholarship exam as a test run — but even if I pass, I don't have to go there. They seem to know what they are doing, but it seems a bit strange to me.

Saturday 8/3/41

After you left Sidway we had the play. It went down very well and we collected 12/6 for the "Spitfire Fund" after-wards. (We now have 17/6). I enclose my report. When I came back from prep on Sunday I found that Walker had cut his hand very badly and now has his arm in a sling. On Monday we drew in the afternoon. I am drawing Sidway.
On Tuesday we shot. I did worse than ever this time. I only got 11. Jill left with Mrs Rigby while we were drawing after shooting (I was going on with the drawing I started on Monday).
On Wednesday we played football and Mr Rigby said that I was playing rather better than usual and our side won. Stamp collecting is still going strong. Please can you send some stamps in your next letter? The sorts I want are as follows:- first choice:- British colonials modern and Victorian, second choice:- Modern colonials. Third choice:- Victorian colonials. fourth choice:- French colonials. Fifth choice:- any stamps you can get hold of.

On Thursday we went for a walk and waged a war against the juniors which we (naturally) won. We had a pillow fight in the dormitory this morning in which the team were Longland, Vaughton, Smith ma. Homer, Griffiths and myself against Ward ma., Darling, Redmayne, Smith min. & Barker. Hinde did not take part as he tore a ligament of his right arm on Tuesday when he tripped up and wrenched it. He also has it in a sling but is now able to write. We are going to take the exam on Wednesday and Thursday this week. We are going to do the Greek paper and the Latin B (loud groans). We are not going to church today.

On Friday we went for a walk and Ward, Darling and Myself pretended we were part of a British invasion of Germany. On Saturday we played football. Thank you for the letter.

P.S. Thanks for coming over on Saturday and Sunday and thanks for the tea (yum yum).

So, we're all set for the exams. Smith and Hinde are taking them too.

Sunday 16/3/41

The exams were held on Wednesday and Thursday as arranged. Yesterday we had a lovely time on the outskirts of a wood. We had a picnic there at Mrs Rigby's suggestion. It was a glorious day and we were at a spot were the trees had been cut down and there was tons of brushwood logs and sticks lying about. We found a sort of gorge about 15 feet across collected tree trunks and put these across supporting the thinner ones with forked branches. We then interlaced these with branches and sticks and then threw bracken to thatch it. It will hold about 10 people and next time we go there were are going to extend it down the gorge. The headroom is about 4ft.

On Friday we had lovely fun pulling logs from the wood with hooks, chains and ropes to the wood shed. In the dorm at night we have been hearing and seeing planes (we looked out of the windows) and have seen flares, searchlights and flashes (source unknown). There must have been some "fire-works" some-where. We will get the results of the exam near the end of May. From what Mr Rigby says I think we have all passed.

Yes, RVR seemed to be very pleased, which is good — because when he isn't his glasses flash and he looks very fierce. You can always tell if he's in a bad mood because he wears those sinister ones with triangular frames. Anyway, Dad has written to say that he thinks I should really try for Oakham School, which sounds like a good idea.

Sunday 30/3/41

Thank you for the stamp hinges and letter. I am glad Oakham is a Rugger school. I have always wanted a crack at the game. I am sorry Dad could not come on the Parents weekend but if he had come it would only have made his chill worse. I hope it is getting better now. Thank you very much for the stamps Mum brought. I enclose an advertisement for some stamps. Please send off the advert just a day or two before I return and please request approvals. (I will fork out for those). I also enclose the names of two stamp collecting friends :- B.C.R.Griffiths, 98 Alcester Road, Moseley, Birmingham13. A.J. Homer, 118 Viceroy Close, Bristol Road, Edgbaston, Birmingham 5. The "Bus" arrives at Hallfield at 12.30 p.m. April 9th.
Holidays April 9th – May 2nd
Please send report back before April 4th. Nothing much happened this week. On Wednesday we played football. A

boy called Boardman has got German Measles. It's a lovely day today and we have been to church. We made a lovely battleship out of cards the other day and Mr Rigby was very pleased with it. We have had a bridge tournament. I have finished "Murder On The Links" it was a very good book. P.S. Thanks for coming over last week end.

Mum wrote to say that she had been ill — flu, I think. Dad has been feeling bad too, but keeps going to the office and has his ARP duties as well. Anyway, I'll be home soon for the Easter holiday and can help a bit.

Sunday 6/4/41

Thank you for the letters. I am glad Dad is feeling better now. It was nice of Auntie Linda to help like that when Mum wasn't too well. The daffodils are now bursting forth in bloom and the drive is looking very gay. I can't find the exam results at the moment, but I will bring them home with me. I don't think I did get a present from Uncle Bob and Auntie Nora. The little boy who sat on the bomb had got a nerve, but I don't think its very plain exactly how and where he got the fins. I have made one or two dates for the Holidays as follows:-

Person	Place	Day	Time
Barker	Five Ways	Next Friday	10 a.m.
Griffiths ma.	Traffic lights	Next	
	Cannon Hill	Thursday	10 a.m.

I hope they will be all right. We have now had all Exams (term and King Edwards). Last Sunday we went to the den and built a stockade around it. as the smaller boys had built dens of their own we used ours as a fort and proceeded accordingly.

We were weighed and measured on Thursday afternoon. My

height is 4ft 10$^{7/8}$ inches. Weight 5 stone 13 lbs. Chest Expansion 3 inches.

On Friday we had a Preliminary for the Elocution Competition and there are 4 boys who are not yet finally chosen for the comp. 2 have got to be picked out and I am one of the four.

On Tuesday there was the shooting comp. I came about 5th. Yesterday Mr Homer kindly came and gave a film show. There was one Laurel and Hardy, a Charlie Chaplin, a Harold Lloyd each of two reels and about 6 reels taken by Mr Homer. There was a collection for the Spitfire Fund afterwards and we now have £1..13s..2½d. We went to church this morning as usual. I have discovered a Levant Stamp in my album catalogued at 35/6d.

The holidays have flashed past as usual..........

Sunday 4/5/41

We arrived safely at Sidway at about 5 o'clock finding myself (you'll be pleased to hear) a prefect. After making a filthy row in the playroom for a bit we had supper (ham) and, after making more row we went to bed. Getting up we went down the following morning to a breakfast of porridge and eggs. We then (to our horror) began work. (We have a new master in place of Mr Woodfine who has left called Mr Shaw).

At length we worked through the morning and then (Oh joy!) came a glorious afternoon, during which we had an even more glorious time. There were three alternatives:- Cycling, Walking and Helping (I helped). the work (most glorious of its kind) was to mow the lawn with a <u>MOTOR-MOWER</u>!

I composed these lines about it:-

O, how glorious to mow with ease,
Round hedges, flowerbeds and trees,
And, on your ebbing strength to bring no toll,
With pulsing monster safely in control.

Mr Rigby taught me how to drive it, and I mowed the lawn with a two stroke single cylinder engine. I was mowing wiggley lines all over the place but after a bit I got more or less used to it. It had a kick-starter and it was lovely fun starting it. I also had a ride when Homer drove Mr Rigby's car when mowing the cricket pitch.

We got up this morning had breakfast and went to Church (Holy Communion). We walked part of the way back and were picked up by Mr and Mrs Rigby.

P.S. Please send <u>aluminium</u> hot water bottle to carry water when going to Den and my little Bible (in my bookcase) and a prayer book.

The aluminium hot water bottle has arrived and it's great for the den. I will be having a picnic, I think, though there isn't much tuck left. Now I'm a prefect, I'm allowed to wear long trousers!

Sunday 11/5/41

Thanks for the letter and the parcel. The dates, cake and sweets will come in very handy. I have got the bible I went away with but it is for school use. (I have got a small bible at home). I never knew I came away to Denstone with a prayer book, at least I never saw one. I enclose the following poem:-

<u>Eventide</u>

The silence of the dorm is shattered,

Floor and walls are bashed and battered,
Boys come in in steady stream,
Silence soon gives way to screams,
Clamour, crashes, clangs and shouts,
Water spilt by clumsy louts,
Silence reigns while prayers are said,
And then the dorm gets into bed,
But soon, however, all is dead,
And slumber droops her sleepy head.

That as you probably gathered was more about the dorm going to bed than "Eventide", but still there it is.

My arm is getting much better thank you, and all the daffodils are out. We went to the den last Sunday and yesterday and climbed lots of trees (I got about 25 feet up one) (swank! swank!). Mr Shaw the new master is awfully decent. While we were at the den we also built a high stockade. We have not been to church today. This afternoon we will either play cricket or go to the den.

We've had some great weather recently — great for 'denning'.

Sunday 18/5/41

Thanks for the letter. Last Sunday afternoon we did play cricket and I managed to get 3 runs. My poetic (??!!) turn of mind has been at work again, and I managed to concoct the following during prep when I had finished my work. Here it is:-

War!

The sorrows of a warring world,
Are felt when banners are unfurled,
Trumpets blare and war drums throb,

Men look grim and women sob.

Men away! Your nations bleeding,
Haste! and to our banner speeding,
Fight the fight of might and right,
Hew a way to freedom's light;*

In reply to your question:- (This was composed in prep so it must have been written more or less on the spot) * <u>There's more of it</u>

Field guns roar and rifles crack,
Many go but few come back,
Fight 'gainst tyrants rank and plane,
Fight! And victory you'll gain.

Well, there it is, it's more like an exhortation than a poem, but you asked for it so you got it!
We played cricket on Wednesday and I got 2, We played yesterday and I got 3 again. We again went to the den on Friday and had the usual picnic. Today we will probably play cricket again. My arm did get a bit worse but its O.K. now. Yes, we heard about Hesse here. Isn't it topping? Yes, Mr Shaw's jolly good as a teacher. My duties as a prefect are not very heavy, but it's a responsibility and I like it.
We are not going to church today as there are measles at Maer.

There should be some news about the King Edwards exams any day now.

Sunday 25/5/41

Thanks for the parcels and letters. The Whitsun Holidays

are Sat May 31st and Sun June 1st. There will be cricket with fathers and if Dad will play so much the better*. Mon. June 2nd. Sun June 22nd is the official father's match.
(*This father's match is not formal. Flannels to be worn if possible).

On Sunday last, after we had written our letters, we went for a walk and saw a glider monoplane being towed by a bi-plane. It looked super. That afternoon we played cricket and I got a "duck". On Monday and Tuesday I was laid up in bed with a temperature feeling "sick-dizzy". I'll go on with the news afterwards.

I enclose the first quarterly report. On Wednesday we went out to play cricket but after about five minutes it started to rain so we went in. And so far it has done that every day of the week since then. It looks pretty awful now. We aren't going to church today as the measles are still on at Maer.

Have you had any more blitzes? I haven't written to Uncle Bob and Auntie Nora yet but I intend to do so after this letter. I haven't finished the book they sent yet. I hope Derek will soon get well, it must be nice at Harrogate. Did Auntie Alice get the fins of the incendiaries that fell on their garden for Derek?

We have lots of bluebells out round here, and we have been picking them for Mrs Rigby and Miss Taylor. We have got a new mistress called Miss Porter who looks a bit like a man-woman. Thanks for Dad's letter it was most inspiring. We had our hair cut a few days ago but it does not affect my strength (Samson)(!??) In the place of my gym vest I am wearing an Aertex one.

We seem to be doing pretty well in Crete.

P.S. Mr Rigby has told me that I have got one of the first five places in King Edwards (Scholarship!) Whoopee!!

Actually, there has been a bit of a stink about the exam results. Smith and Hinde were taking the exam too and all of us got top places (Smith came first, Hinde was second and I came third). then RVR had to tell King Edwards that none of us wanted to take up the scholarship places — Smith is wanting to go to Bromsgrove, Hinde is keen on Malvern and I'm going to try for Oakham. It seems that the head of King Edward's was furious. What a lark!

Sunday 8/6/41

Thanks for the letter and the B.O.P. My exam will take place tomorrow, Tuesday, Wednesday and one on Thursday. I just sent up for some approvals sheets and got some fairly nice stamps. I enclose a tooth I pulled out last night after lights-out and it bled like anything. I also enclose a notice about the Fathers' cricket match and the Sports.

We did not go to church this Sunday but we will go next Sunday. Yesterday we played cricket and I made one run, let through 2 byes at wicket and caught one boy out. Yesterday there was a match against the King Edwards Juniors at Hallfield and we beat them by 9 wickets. They got 39 runs. On Friday we went to the den and had a picnic. On Thursday it rained so Hinde and myself played duets on the piano.

We have had no air raids over here at all. I am glad Derek's getting better.

My wars (imaginary) are getting on fine but enemy parachutists are doing a lot of damage to communications and material.

On Wednesday we played cricket and I got 3. On Tuesday I went for a walk. Its just beginning to rain and I don't think we shall go out.

I won't be here at Sidway for very much longer and it will be a shame to say goodbye to the den. but the next hurdle is an exam for Oakham and that's coming very soon.

Sunday 15/6/41

I enclose my exam papers, my second quarterly report and another piece of paper on which is drawn a flag. The flag is for a den built by Smith, Barker and myself; hence S I B. I would be very much obliged if you could make it sometime (as early as poss.) out of the odds and ends in the bottom drawer of my dressing table.

We have found a slender fallen pine tree near our den's outpost about 30 ft high. On Saturday when we went I took off my shirt tied it to the top of the pine and lashed it to a dead, stunted, straight pine tree about 20 feet high. Here is a good piece of news, Vaughton, a Hallfield boy may be going to Oakham. The Oakham papers were pretty stiff especially the Greek and Latin Translation; the rest were O.K. A Match was played at Hallfield yesterday against "George Dixon's" and we lost by 13 runs to 140. It's the best prep school team in Birmingham.

We did not go to church today either as the measles is still hanging about. I see from a notice on the notice board that Dad is playing in the match. I bet he gets a duck. On Monday we were kept in for making a row in the dorm. I made a mistake about exams they began on Tuesday and finished on Thursday. On Friday and Saturday we went "denning".

The weather's a lot better again. We are having to play heaps of cricket, but I'm not as good as some of the others.

Monday 16/6/41

I thought I'd just drop you a line because there's something I forgot in my last letter. Please could you bring my printing set (consisting of an empty honey jar full of type and a green box plainly marked "Printing Set") which is in my cabinet, with you when you come on the "Parent's Weekend" and a bottle of Indian ink and a bottle of red ink. On Sunday afternoon we played cricket and when I was keeping wicket a ball bowled by Pfeil caught me full on the chin. I did not melt into tears (swank! swank!) but it's left a lovely grazed dark purple bruise.

Mr Green my violin master has been away for some weeks, as one of two brackets holding the engine to the chassis broke and he ran 5,000 miles with his engine at an angle to the horizontal.

I think Mr. Green's car is a bit of a wreck, really. He often has trouble starting it and it smokes a lot. Mum was worried about me being hit by that cricket ball and asked if my teeth were OK. It was nothing really and I wish I hadn't mentioned it. We're having a heat wave and it seems to be even worse in Birmingham.

Sunday 29/6/41

Thanks for the BO.P., the letters and aeroplane disc. I have received a letter from Uncle Bob and Auntie Nora complete with a 2/6 postal order. If I have time after this letter I will write them one. I have replied to Nana's letter. On Monday we had a gooseberry picking contest; the idea was to pick more gooseberries than anyone else. There were five pairs of boys, Smith ma. and myself, Griffiths ma. and Pfeil, Redmayne and Barker, Ward and Darling, Smith min. and Walker. The prize was 6d each for the boys in the first pair.

5d for the second, 4d for the third, and so on. Smith ma. and myself carried off the first prize with four big plant pots full off gooseberries between us. Altogether 121 lbs of fruit were picked. On Wednesday and Thursday we had to "top and tail" them; and we also picked the dead flowers off the violas in the rose-garden. On Tuesday we played Maer at cricket a game in which I (for once) took part. They went in first and scored 23 all out. Then we went in and got 94 for 3 declared, and so I never got an innings. On Friday we went for a walk to the Roman Camp where we had a picnic tea. On Saturday we played Broughton Hall here but were beaten although some very good catches were taken by our fielders. I did not play in that match (that's why we lost). The final score was we:- 67 all out; they:- 87 all out.

This morning we went to church and I took my prayer book. The heat has gone now so it can't be so fatiguing any more. I have not received the book club book yet. Mr Rigby has acquired a Labrador retriever, it's a beauty and it's very obedient (like me ??!!).

Not much longer till the end of term now.

Sunday 6/7/41

On Sunday afternoon we played cricket and I got a duck. On Monday we had to work hard, had no tuck or jam, and the prefects deprived of their power, because we talked a lot on Sunday night (I'm not complaining because we asked for it). The prefects were deprived of their duties etc., for not stopping the row.

On Tuesday we had the half holiday to which we were entitled (scholarship) and played cricket. (I made 6).

On Wednesday we went swimming in the Tern and had a lovely time except that poor Walker gashed his left knee open on a jagged brick. He had to have a stitch in it.

On Thursday we went for a walk and bombarded Mr Shaw with ferns pulled out by the roots and stripped of their leaves. (We used them like javelins).

On Friday we went to the Roman Camp and had a good time.

On Saturday we played cricket and had 2 innings. I got 3; 0 respectively.

Today we went to church.

Thank you for the letters and stamps.

P.S. We saw a huge dragonfly on Saturday about four inches long.

I enclose my third quarterly report. One of the boys here collects autographs. He must be completely barmy. He's writing to the King and "Winnie" for their autographs.

Some of us have had some fun putting together news items for our own paper, the 'Sidway News'. I hoped I could do something for it with my printing set, but it didn't work well enough.

Saturday 12/7/41

Thanks for the letter and quarterly report. I enclose a copy of the "Sidway News". Also the rough M.S. of an article I am writing for the "Hallfieldian", sub-edited by Mr Shaw; and I have now written a copy of it complete with corrections. On Monday Homer and myself cleaned Mr Rigby's car and got ourselves soaking wet. On Tuesday we played a game with Maer; you can see the results in the Stop Press of the "Sidway News". On Wednesday there was an away match with Broughton Hall. We lost:- we 33 they 141 for 8 declared. On Thursday we went for a walk with Mr Shaw. On Friday we went to the roman camp, which is beyond the den. On Saturday we had the Nowers and Pughe match. Pughe won:- 81 for 9 declared to 56. I got 4 runs and let through 4 byes at wicket. This morning we went to church.

We are coming to Hallfield on Saturday next, July 19th, arriving in time for the sports at 2.30 p.m. We shall have an early lunch at Sidway before we start. We will have a picnic tea with our parents on the field at 4.30 p.m. If you are not able to give tea will you please let Mr Rigby know? On 26th July term ends. We will break up in the gym at Hallfield 11.30 – 12.30. I have sent a letter to Stanley Gibbons for some stamps. It is rather hot here but the heat is not really affecting us. The Tern is not a lake it's a river; you know, the place where we went for a walk. Mr Shaw was not at all wild he took it as a joke. The dragonfly was not blue or green, it was brown and with yellow stripes. We have had some bad thunder recently. Have you had any? I have heard that you had a practice invasion on Saturday night at "Brum". What was it like?

P.S. Walker has had his stitch taken out. I have finished the Book Club Book.

THE DEN

One glorious afternoon, during our first term at Sidway, we set out to the Maer woods. After we had been walking for half and hour or so we arrived at a spot where woodmen cut town trees over a large area, now littered with branches and brushwood. We immediately hit on the idea of building a den out of this debris, and chose the site, a narrow dip about 8 feet deep 12 feet wide, and 100 yards long. Working in gangs we scavenged the whole area and soon collected up several logs, left by the (lumbermen) woodcutters. We set these across the dip, and covered them up with smaller branches and brushwood. After a picnic tea we returned home, pleased with a hard day's work.

The following Saturday afternoon we returned, only to find

that the main support had cracked and that the whole roof had fallen in under the strain. Undaunted, we hauled out the tangled wreckage of our labour. We went out in larger gangs; brought back more massive logs set them across our miniature ravine and this time made doubly sure of the den's strength by propping up the logs with large forked branches. Then we covered our "house" in exactly the same way as before. There was still a large portion left open to the sky, but the bare framework was completed. this was soon covered over on our next visit. (We were engineers).

G.N.Iley

So, it's the Summer holiday again and goodbye to Sidway. Mum and Dad took me on a picnic in the country. It was a lovely day and Dad took a photo.

3. Long trousers on a picnic!

In no time at all, I'll be starting at Oakham. This time I shall be going by train from New Street station, which will be a change from that rickety old bus. There will be a different school uniform and lots of different rules. I think I'm going to like it OK, but it's difficult to know what to expect.

Autumn 1941 — Summer 1942

Wharflands
Oakham School
Rutland

Sunday 21/9/41

I have settled down quite nicely now. I am sharing with a boy called Mason, and later on with Abbot as well. They have a novel system of rent here for studies, paid to the last occupants; this amount varies with each study and ours is 3/- per head of occupants. Any old curtains will do for "tappo" (tapestry), and I have purchased some drawing pins to put it up with. Our study is now furnished with:- a piece of "tappo" 2' x 2' (approx.) 3d; two tuck boxes, a table (covered with my rug), and a piece of carpet 6' x 3' in good condition auctioned to me for 6½d, and a chair auctioned to me for 10d. In fact it's more or less sorted itself out now. I have also got a lucky horseshoe bought for 1d. "Tappo" is also used as wallpaper so please send it "en masse" and not in narrow strips. I am managing my collar all right and have lost no studs yet.

There is fagging here but luckily there are 7 new boys and 4 prefects to fag for and I have not been pounced on yet. We make our beds every other morning, and we made ours today. I am in the lower V and am taught by "Wily Willie" Watts. There was no prep last night and there is none on Sundays. We went to chapel yesterday and are going today; the service is not bad but the chants (i.e. The lord be with you:- And with thy spirit) are sung to strange tunes. The

food is all right, but they never sugar your tea or coffee (you have a choice of tea or coffee at breakfast). There are weird rules in connection with seniors (i.e. Boys who have studies in the house), but I can't go into those at length at the moment.

Actually, it's not too bad here. I like sharing a study in the hut. This is a big wooden building just outside the main part of Wharflands, with a common room at one end heated by on old 'Tortoise' stove that burns coke. Then at the other end there are six studies grouped around a second stove.

It's all very different of course and the rules seem a bit strange and strict, but I'm sure I'll get used to it in time. I know it's wartime and we can't expect the food to be wonderful, but Sidway was pretty good really. There is one good thing, though. The dining hall in my house, Wharflands, has a big dresser on one side and every boy (there are 44 of us) has his own saucer with his name on it. These are for our personal share of the weekly butter and margarine ration, after the kitchen has taken some off for cooking. There are two tiny bits about the size of a matchbox. Anyone who pinches anybody else's ration gets KILLED!

Sunday 28/9/41

Thank you very much for the presents and things. It is raining lions and tigers at the moment. So far I have had £1-10-6 in cash and P.O's. With part of the money I have bought a cheap plane kit and am making it at the moment. I have joined the scouts but discipline is awfully slack and it is hardly worth going. I have played Rugger and like it very much, but I have not scored any tries yet. I have had a medical inspection and have had my ears syringed a huge lump of wax came out of my left ear.

Our study is looking very nice now we've got the curtains up. Please will you send the name and address of our family doctor the matron wants to know. Please write once or twice a week, as you think best. I am too young to go into the O.T.C. but I am learning to play the bugle, it's wizard fun. We are often being raided by the dorm above and we have super fights. The Anzac biscuit and cake are awfully nice. Here are some of the rules:-

Always give way to someone with a study in the house.
Always stand up   "   "   "   "   "
Always keep your coat buttoned.
Always open the door to a senior.
Run baths for seniors.
Clean out studies belonging to seniors.
Take down black out in   "   "   "

The parents seem to be a bit peeved because I'm not telling them stuff that they want to know. Dad's even sent me a questionnaire!

Thursday 9/10/41

I am sorry I have not written earlier, but I have been in the "San" since Sunday afternoon with a bad headache, a temperature and feeling rotten. I am all right now though.
I have got some good news for you. I have met a Mr Wrigley who we used to know at Lincoln here, when I went to the Midland Bank to cash a cheque. He sends a note and his kind regards.
You will probably be annoyed to hear that I have bought a good camera, a folding one. It should have been 32/6 but the people there brought it down to 25/- for me. I enclose some snaps I have taken.
I enclose 2 postal orders for savings. I have seen the very

sort of wireless book in Oakham that I want and intend to buy it. I hope this is O.K. by you. I am playing oodles of chess with Beecroft. The seniors are on the whole pretty decent. Here are some rules I forgot.

You must have all your coat buttons done up.
You must not sing or whistle
You must ask the prefect in charge of Prep when you come back from a bath if you can do your hair.

The "Hallfieldian" has arrived now and when you come over for a visit I will let you have it. It's rather good about the increased rations. The extra sugar will come in handy for you. The 6 collars are enough thanks. The Stamp album is fine thanks.

I am fagging for a prefect called O'Hagan and he says I am very good at making cocoa. We played the Old Boys at Rugger last Saturday and licked them 25 points to nil. Pretty hot eh!

P.S. If you have time will you please make some elderberry wine.

O'Hagan is actually quite easygoing apart from one or two routine things (like making cocoa and doing toast round the old cast iron stove in the common room at the top of the hut). He plays Rugger for the first XV and I have to clean his muddy boots and take him his cocoa in the changing room after a game. A whole gang of them sit up to their necks in a huge bath with scalding hot water while they drink cocoa and sing. Some of the words are very rude.

The only bad thing about fagging is that sometimes a prefect who wants a job done, or a message delivered will come into the top of the hut and shout 'FAG' and then we all have to come running. The one who arrives last gets the task (and if you try to hide or pretend you didn't hear, then you get into serious trouble).

Sunday 19/10/41

I am sorry I am so long in writing, but nothing very exciting happened between last Thursday and Sunday.

You wanted more details about the San. Here they are. It is a very old building built by two monks in about 1000 A.D. The matron Miss Battershall is rather deaf but very nice indeed. I read oodles of books during my stay there and had a pretty good time on the whole. I had a sleeping draught for the first time there.

On Tuesday we had a field day in which the Scouts took part. We played a "wide" game; that is, a game spread over an area of a square mile or so. It was the object of everybody to capture people of the other side (by force). The trouble was that just as we were going to have a pitched battle between the main forces of both sides, the whistle went for time.

Thank you very much indeed for the chair, tablecloth etc.

I am afraid sweets are running rather low now but jams are O.K.

Please will you send my scout uniform, socks, woggle, scarf, garter, tabs, belt, and any such paraphernalia there may be hanging about. Please could you get me a blue and grey shoulder ribbon. The only other thing I need is a scout hat (the other got left at Denstone).

Yesterday we played Stamford School in three games and lost them all.

Mum and Dad have gone to Southport to stay with old friends from the Bank. They've known 'Uncle' Bob and 'Auntie' Ethel Hampshire for ages and ages and we had a great holiday with them and their son Bill on the Norfolk Broads when I was about eight.

Sunday 26/10/41

Thank you for the letter. I hope you are enjoying your stay at Southport. There is not much to write about this week really, but here goes.

I can now play "All for a shilling a day" on the bugle and also "Fall in".

I have been getting into hot water lately, I forgot to put up O'Hagan's blackout the other night and narrowly missed a tanning for it. I also got told off twice on the same day as the black out incident for other things. Here is a 'pome' on the sort of life I lead here.

<u>School Life at Oakham</u>

You wake up in the morning with your eyelids made of lead,
Then someone says "get up there!" and blips you on the head,
You charge downstairs to find you're late,
And then await your awful fate;
And so you hare round to the place*
Where the prefects wait en masse.
Getting three, you're jolly sore,
Then "late for beds!" * you get some more,**
In school lessons lines are meted out,
And people call "you clumsy lout!",
At last to bed you slowly climb,
Strongly hoping all the time,
That by tomorrow's dawning light,
The prefect's cuts will lose their bite.

* pronounced "plass"
**we make our beds in the morning

Its getting rather cold now, and we have been given our winter underwear. I have got some little spots under my arm but they are going down now. I have nearly passed my tenderfoot now and hope to get it next time. I'm sorry this letter is so short, but I have been writing thank you letters etc., and also have some impots to do.

* * *

Sunday 2/11/41

Thanks very much for the parcels letters etc. the chair has now come and it is very comfortable. As you see from the address I am now in the San again. I have contracted Shingles or something of the sort which seems to be a most peculiar disease; I have spots under my right armpit and spots on my nose. I feel perfectly well, but they have put me in here because I can give other boys chicken-pox (rather peculiar, what?). I have got oodles of time on my hands, and can wonder freely about the town, and don't have to stay in bed.

The san was first built in 10- by two monks from Westminster Abbey, and was used as a very small, poor monastery. After two wings were added in 15- it was used as a vicarage until the School bought it in 1890, and shortly after the last war the other wing was built of old stone in 1920.

You will be pleased to hear that I got my tenderfoot last Tuesday, the day before I came into the San.

I forgot in my last letter to tell you that we had two air raids during the week, but we did not go to the shelters and no bombs were dropped, although we did have some planes go over.

The tuck was very welcome; that piece of rock was the first I've seen for about a year I should think.

I can now hear Lane (a pal of mine) practising the organ in the chapel. He's awfully good at it. Furley and Hassan are completely out of Scout gear and so I won't be able to get anything here in that line.

I have been popping in and out of wireless shops here and this is more or less the procedure:—

Enter Geoffrey:-

Geoffrey: (trying to appear important) Excuse me, but do you sell circuits here?

Bert (to Harold): 'Arry, does we sell circuits 'ere?

Harold (to Bill): Bill, does we sell circuits 'ere?

Bill (to Harold): Noa!

Harold (to Bert): Noa!

Bert: Noa!

Geoffrey (slightly put out): Oh! (exits).

I am sorry, but I don't know anything about the belt.

* * *

Tuesday 11/11/41

I am sorry I did not write on Sunday, but I did not seem to have time, as I had to do Photography. We have now made several prints and enlargements. On Saturday we had a Camp Fire (Scout term for a "do") and acted plays, it coming off much better than was expected. In fact, a good time was had by all. I am getting on fine at scouts now and have passed 3 out of the 8 Second-Class tests.

This afternoon we were clearing a path that had been overgrown, and have made (if I may say so) a pretty good job of it. This letter is I know, very scrappy, but I have not much time nowadays to write letters at all and goodness knows when I'll finish off my thank you letters. I am now playing games again and am more or less O.K. I was very glad to see you the other weekend and the cake etc., was very nice. I'll have to finish off now or I won't catch the post, so Goodbye.

* * *

Sunday 23/11/41

Thanks for the letters. we had a match yesterday against the R.A.F. Syston, but lost 11 – 4.
The weather has been fairly good lately, and I have been out for walks in the surrounding country, and dug up an interesting fact. Here it is:- about the time of the industrial revolution a canal was built from the place where the quadrangle now is to Stamford and was going to be carried on to Peterborough, but the company went smash and they filled it in. Hence the name "Wharflands". There are some old wharf houses a few hundred yards away and so one day I went and nosed round, but they were not very interesting. Here are some answers to Dad's photography questions. The enlarger is rather old fashioned, originally intended for plates and gas, but adapted to electricity and is liable to give electric shocks. We enlarge onto Gaslight papers, and use Metol-quinal developer and Acid hypo fixing. We have dug up an old plate of a factory called (or at) Gwershafen Siegfried and wonder if it has Military importance.
I have passed for second class the following tests, (i) Compass, (ii) Signalling, (iii) First aid. I have yet to do (i)

knots and lashings, (ii) 1 months service, (iii) observation, (iv) light a fire in the open, (v) knifeman and axemanship. The debating society is open to seniors, but juniors may speak when it is declared open to the house. I hope Uncle Tom will have better luck with his house hunting. I have read "Deep Down" by Ballantyne and soon hope to get my second reader badge.

* * *

Sunday 30/11/41

Thanks for the letters. It is very cold today and does not feel like an afternoon for going out. I am studying for the Miner badge (know the workings of our particular branch of the mining industry, know the dangers, and safety measures) also the Electricians badge and the Missioners badge. Requirements for the reader badge are :- Have read 18 good books in the past 12 months, and know their theme and general outline.

We played the R.A.F. yesterday and won 10 – 12. I think Dad's suggestion about the Everyman's Library (boy's section) seems pretty good, and I think I would rather have those than the Childrens' Book Club. For goodness sake don't send the kid gloves or I shall die of shame.

For second class signalling you need to know the semaphore or morse sign for every letter in the alphabet and for the numerals, and be able to send and read a simple message. The operator must understand the use of the calling up sign, and its answer, the general answer, the end of the message sign and its answer, and the erase signal.

We have had the third quarterly report and I dropped, I am sorry to say, from 9th to 13th but I have been getting very much higher marks since the order has been given, and I hope it will continue.

Isn't it good about Libya, General Rommel seems to be getting it good and proper this time, and we seem to stand a good chance of getting Tripoli. We have had no more air raids, and I hope that you have been equally free from them.

I have just remembered it's nearly Dad's birthday. What on earth can I get him that doesn't cost too much? The parents seem to be a bit worried about arrangements for coming home for the holidays, but the rail journey shouldn't be any problem really.

Saturday 6/12/41

Dear Dad,

Many happy returns of the day. I hope you will like the enclosed present of a bookmark. I am afraid it is not very much to look at, but it was all I could afford, and am now down to 3½d.

I think I will be able to manage all the journey on my own, and I will come back on the 9.02 from Oakham. There will be no need to write to Mr Goodchild about arrangements as we are expected to manage them by ourselves; but could you please send the required for a ticket as, as I have mentioned above, funds are running rather low.

Uncle Tom seems to have an interesting job. I hope his idea for a new needle will work out all right. I will write more fully on Sunday as I have not time now.

Uncle Tom is one of my favourite Uncles. He does lots of engineering things, training apprentices for the war effort. I like the sound of his job.

Sunday 7/12/41

Thank you for the letters and things that have arrived during the week. I hope Dad likes the present of the Bookmark.

The weather here is quite fine, and the sun is doing its best, but the wind is largely nullifying its effect.

From what I can make out, one goes gay on the last day of term. (It's an old Spanish Custom) wearing purple and green ties with orange spots, and so forth. I wonder if you could oblige with a flashy tie and handkerchief to decorate myself with. I should think Mum has a gaily coloured handkerchief somewhere, and Dad probably has a nice blue-murdery tie. If not, I hope I can secure one, or both, during the holidays to wear for the next homecoming. Could you please send a stamp for my next letter, as I am almost completely broke.

There is, every winter term, a Darts, Billiards and Ping Pong competition; unfortunately I was knocked out of every one in the first round, but I hope I won't do so badly next year.

We played R.A.F. yesterday at Rugger in driving rain, and drew 11 – 11, although the R.A.F. had a Rugby International playing for them. (His name is Walker, and he is the world's best fly-half).

I have some good news about the Scouts:- I may get made a Patrol Second, as the proper one has been rather playing the fool lately.

I have discovered two books in the Library simply bung full of radio circuits, and I will come home loaded up to the eyelids with same.

I managed to get Mum a little brooch for her birthday. I hope she likes it. We have all heard about the Japanese attack on Pearl Harbour. The Americans are sure to react and I expect they will be fighting the Germans too, which is good news for us.

Thursday 11/12/41

Thanks very much for the letters. Many happy returns of the day, Mum. I hope this gets to you in time for your birthday and hope you will like it. I have not much time to write, but am just sending you a note as it is nearly teatime. I will have to close now.

* * *

Sunday 14/12/41

Thank you for the letters. This week has been rather crowded, so I think I had better write the letter in diary form:-

Monday: Same as usual. Saw Cottesmore hunt riding down Station Street.

Tuesday: Same as usual. Played Rugger.

Wednesday: Last period of morning spent practicing for the carol service. Good time was had by all.

Thursday: Last game of Rugger this term.

Friday: Last Scout parade.

Saturday: Went to the Regent and saw "Target for Tonight" again, second and third periods of morning. Match in the afternoon (under 14) against Kingswood; lost by us 15 – 0. Saw film in the evening (talkie) at the drawing school. It was quite good; "The Good Companions" by J.B.Priestley.

Today we went to chapel as usual. It is raining now and the weather looks rather depressing. We are having a grand time in lessons now, we are being read to by Mr Watts from a book of short stories. On Thursday we will have what is known as a "Gut" (i.e. feast) followed by dorm plays. There will be an under 14 concert tonight at 6, in which I luckily will not take part. I will be able to get a monthly return as we go back on the 16th of January.

Home for Christmas! The big news is that the Americans are actually at war with Germany too — that should make things a lot better for us here in Europe.

We had the usual festivities and Dad managed to get a turkey, but it wasn't very big. We went to an ARP party on the Pineapple Road estate. It was a lot of fun and I learned to do the 'Hokey Kokey'.

Sunday 18/1/42

You will be pleased to hear that I am round the stove, have moved up two studies, am head of the dorm, and will be off fagging.

I arrived safely at about 3.10 and saw about the ticket. They told me to call again in a week's time after I have filled up a form.

Richardson is now dorm prefect and is (as far as I can make out) jolly decent.

I am still in lower V. No new boys have come up into our form but there are four new boys in Wharflands:- Snipper (from Junior House) Hopewell & Pennington (from Magnus) and Bowman (from some school at Stamford).

We went to Chapel today as usual and had a more or less usual service.

Please do you think you could send a small remittance to keep me going until ticket cashes in; what with rent and what-not I'm rather low in money.

P.S. I feel much more at home now and more like "one of the mob".

As well as being in the Scouts I'm still practising the bugle so that when I eventually join the O.T.C. I can be in the Drums — the proper name is the Drum Corps — there's lots of drums, naturally, plus about eight fifes and six buglers.

Sunday 25/1/42

Thanks for your letters. I am settling in fine, and can do prep in my study.

Heavy snow fell overnight on Tuesday, but it has now nearly all gone because of heavy rain which fell on Friday.

On Thursday I had a simply marvellous time in the afternoon, as I went sledging on Brook Hill. I came back with aching legs ice on my trousers and inside my coat sleeves, my neck saturated, and my gloves frozen stiff. I luckily suffered no ill effects. Once I went down the hill (almost ¼ mile run) and nearly went into the hedge (I was about 10 yards away).

Lane has brought back a game of Monopoly. I have played twice, losing one game and winning another. I have finished the "Crime and Detection" book now.

The sandwich in the train was fine thanks. I have found the pair of shoes I left. I have had some of the tuck and it was jolly good. I hope you are all O.K. and keeping well.

* * *

Monday 2/2/42

Thank you very much for your letters. And thanks very much for the diary and P.O.

I am very sorry I did not write on Sunday, but I had to go to a meeting of the Musical Society in the afternoon and a concert in the evening. (I am now a member of the afore-mentioned Musical Society).

I hope I have enough time to finish this letter properly but

I am writing it in prep, and I don't know if I will.

You will probably be pleased to hear that I am now a Patrol Second, and am now eligible to join the P.L's parliament of "The Scout".

I'm afraid that I don't need the balaclava, but I'll hang on to it until the end of term. We have had more and more snow here, and had an organised snow fight today, and one yesterday.

I have now got the refund on the ticket and the money has proved a very useful stand-by. Do you think it would be possible to obtain a 6-20 film in Birmingham? You can't get any here. (For goodness sake don't ask for 2¼" x 3¼", they are the wrong size!)

I have drawn blood at boxing, during a round with a boy called Day. I made his nose bleed.

My stomach still seems to be in working order, and I have not had any more trouble.

On Monday last we played Rugger, but had a simply awful game, although I managed to score a try. The final score was 3 – 3.

The study is O.K. now, and I am well settled in, and I am still sharing with Mason.

I am still doing some work and hope to improve my position this time.

I am rehearsing the "Messiah" and making some fairly good "rendings",

I have not had to use the quotation book in work yet, but it is nice to dabble in.

You will be pleased to hear that I have successfully made a scale model plane.

* * *

Monday 9/2/42

I am sorry I did not write as early as usual this week, but I felt rather groggy on Sunday and had to go to bed, but I am up and O.K. now. I had a very big stye on my left eye and a cough and a cold.

Thanks very much indeed for the film, I took four snaps on Sunday. Thanks also for your letter.

On Thursday and Sunday I went sledging at Brook Hill and had a marvellous time. It was a lovely sunny day, and I took (as I have mentioned before) 4 photographs, 2 were of smashes, 1 of a boy going at the dickens of a speed over a jump, and the other of some people going down on a sledge. It is beginning to thaw now, and it is very wet. I have read Coral Island and think it a very good book indeed.

At long last "Wireless for Beginners" will arrive next week in the stationers. I have had it on order for 12 weeks or so.

Do you think you could send a small remittance please? Because after I have bought the book I shall have exactly 4d left.

I got on well at boxing on Saturday, and except for the fact that my upper lip was split in two places, and that my jaw was nearly dislocated (it is still aching) I had quite a nice time.

Oh crikey, what have I done? Perhaps what I said about the boxing in my last letter was a bit dramatic. Anyway, Mum got a bit upset and phoned Wharflands. I was in big trouble, so it seemed like a good idea to send a telegram.

TELEGRAM
10.55 OAKHAM TUESDAY 10-02-42
MR AND MRS ILEY 64 SHUTLOCK LANE BIRMINGHAM13

= AM OK DON'T WORRY STOP WILL WRITE SOON
= GEOFFREY

Sunday 15/02/42

I am sorry I did not write sooner, but here are the reasons.
On Sunday afternoon I did some surveying for the Explorer
Badge (an extremely good badge to have, by the way) and in
the evening did some prep. On Monday I had a music lesson
(which cuts 1½ hours out of prep) and more prep than usual.
On Tuesday I sent the telegram (which I hope relieved your
forebodings. I got in rather a row when you rang up Mrs
Bowes) and in the afternoon had scouts, after which I
managed to write a portion of this letter and had no more
time in prep, but did not manage to finish it on Wednesday,
but today (Sunday) I managed to get it off my chest, as I had
had no other time during the week.

Sunday: Here is some good news. Except for scout's pace
which I have not had time for yet, I have passed the Second
Class badge. I hope to get it finally during the week.

Wednesday: Snow fell here on Saturday, when I went out
with Abbot and had tea at the Crown.

I have a proposition to make re Abbot. If you will let me I
would like to camp out a night or two with him (his parents
are in agreement). He lives at Nottingham but we both
possess bikes, and I think it could be arranged to meet
somewhere.

Thursday: Thanks very much for your letters, but you have
made me feel an awful rotter for not writing sooner, but the
junior steeplechase is today and I have been training for it
as well as swotting for the exams (that's why I have not had
time in prep) which are on Monday.

Thanks also for the P.O. I have added up my expenses and
they come to about 16/-. (Those that I can remember) I lost

heavily on the rent as we paid out for the study we moved into (4/6) and <u>should</u> have received (3/-) rent from the boys who moved into our old one, but Mr Goodchild found out, and put a stop to it.

I have been more or less dieting in preparation for the steeplechase, a long distance run of about four miles and will have a lovely blow out at teatime.

I had tea with Mrs Bowes yesterday with bread and butter, jam and treacle, scones, cream buns and cake. The only snag was that I could not eat much because of the steeplechase. I had a very nice time and played "happy families" and dominoes after tea.

You may come to see me any Sunday you please (if you let me know in advance) as there is no long Sunday this term.

Sweets are running rather low, but the jam etc., will last me the term.

Thanks for the Irish Stamp. the Hallfieldian came O.K. enclosing a polite request for dibs in payment.

No more news as we are going into chapel in a minute.

I missed out on writing for a week or so and got another very shirty letter from Dad. I think he was extra peeved because of the Japs capturing Singapore, which is terrible news for us.

Anyway, Mum and Dad came over for a week end and stayed at The Crown and apart from a good ticking off, we had a good time. I showed them around the town, though there wasn't much to see except the castle, which is quite interesting.

Sunday 22/3/42

Thanks very much for the letter and the tie.

I am sorry I did not write any more last Thursday or Sunday but I had a lot of English to do and did not have time.

On Tuesday we had a field-day, and we had marvellous fun

playing wide games. The best one was a game in which a message was hidden on your person and you had to try and run a blockade. I managed to get through after a little chase. We began tests for the sports on Monday but so far I have not been able to get one:

100 yards 13 secs. I was 2 or 3 secs out.
220 yards 31 secs. I was about 5 secs out.
440 yards 73 secs. I was about 7 secs out.
The 880 yards, long jump and high jump are yet to go, but I doubt if I will get a test, and if I don't, I lose a point for the house. (Long jump 13′ 10″. High Jump 3′ 10″)

Yesterday night we went to the old school and had a talk by a Captain Knight on Eagles. (He is the uncle of Esmond Knight, the actor). He brought with him Mr Ranshaw his pet eagle, who was very tame, and I managed to stroke it. He had taken many films of eagles and showed us some, with a very clever running commentary. One of them was a Melodrama (old style) with Mr Ranshaw as the villain and Esmond Knight as the hero. It was extremely funny.
We had the confirmation on Saturday. I enclose the sheets that we were given. I will go to F & H's and get the cricket shirt.
The Crocuses are all out here and look very nice.

* * *

Thursday 26/3/42

Thanks very much for the letter and the enclosed 10/- note. I am sorry I forgot to enclose the service and I enclose it this time (I hope) but I am writing this letter in fits and starts and may forget it.

About the camping with Abbot, I hope to be able to go over on the 4th of April (the Saturday after I come back) and we will meet at a village about 20 miles S.W. of Nottingham, around noon. I am sure I can find my way by map as I have done it in Birmingham from <u>memory</u> when I went to Robin's and there were <u>thousands</u> of turnings. As for the tent, it won't leak all that much and I can take it anyway. Please write and tell me if this will be all right if there is time.

If you agree could you please collect the following necessary camping articles:-

An axe (I can get it sharpened at Dunbar's)
2 Billy cans (1 with frying pan lid)
1 Box of Matches
1 Tea Infuser
1 Enamel plate (1 mug. I've got one here)
1 Fork 1 knife 1 spoon 1 tea spoon
1 Sleeping bag (that thing I slept in the garden in)
1 Oilskin cape (this will serve the double purpose of a groundsheet as well. I think it is in the garage)

I can settle the rest when I come back.
I will come on the 9.02 as arranged but I have not got the ticket yet.
I forgot to tell you that last week we had Warship week and the Corps took part in the parade, including the Drums (technical name of the corps band). It was a grand sight and they were complimented afterwards by Admiral somebody or other. Last weekend will be one I shall remember all my life, as it was a great occasion for me. On Saturday, as the head bugler was in the San, I was Commandeered by the Corps to play in The Retreat outside Furley and Hassan's on the Bugle. I had never played in the Drums before, but I was

issued with a uniform and although I hardly knew any drill, was complimented afterwards. Said he, blowing his own bugle. (Joke)

On Sunday I played in the "Messiah" and got more or less left behind, but I managed to jog along somehow. The Head man said afterwards that he had never been so moved by anything as he was by that rend(er)ing of the "Messiah".

We had sports yesterday although it was rather cold and windy, and Wharflands won in the Junior Sports, but lost in the Senior sports.

I don't think there is any more news now except that this will be the last time I will write (goody-goody) and I am looking forward to coming home.

Home for the holidays again, but the train was a bit late getting to Birmingham. Dad has an ARP friend called Mr Daw, He lives round the corner in Seaton Grove. I've met him a few times and he told me he has a factory in the centre of Birmingham, near the Hippodrome Theatre. I asked him if I could work there for a few days in the holidays and Dad agreed. So I went there for a whole week, which was interesting, but also rather boring. I had to use a special machine to cut circles about twelve inches in diameter from square sheets of steel. The discs were taken to lathes, where skilled men moulded them onto accurate formers to make circular trays, hubcaps for cars and dishes. The men were very funny and talked about football all the time. Mr.Daw gave me ten shillings at the end of the week, which was jolly decent of him.

I also spent lots of time at the ice rink and made friends with a few people. The time was all too short before I was back on the train again with a packet of chicken and chutney sandwiches — my favourite.

Sunday 3/5/42

I arrived safely in Oakham at about 5 to 3 after a pleasant and feeding journey.

I went to Furley and Hassan's but the smallest straw hats they have are $7^{1/8}$ and that size comes down over my ears. I managed to secure a pair of trousers and a coat though.

We are still in the same studies and the unoccupied study in the Hut has been opened. However, I am now in the upper 12 dormitory. I am still on the same table in the dining hall. I have not seen about a new scout uniform yet.

The battery for my wireless has run out. I can't get a good earth or aerial here so I don't think I will start on it this term.

In school on Saturday we didn't do any work at all worth mentioning.

Tuesday: On Sunday I am afraid I (honestly, Scout's honour etc.) could not finish the letter as I had to clean my corps uniform and march around the town with the drums. In the evening there was a house game of rounders and I am afraid I could not manage to squeeze in the rest of the letter.

I managed to get a Penguin problems book (like the one we once had, that Auntie Betty has got) price 9d. Apart from that there have been no expenses yet, but tonight I will have to fork out my Musical Society subscription of 1/6.

* * *

Thursday 14/5/42

I am sorry I have not written sooner, but here is my letter. please could you send my rugger trousers, as I need them for P.T. which I forgot when I was at home.

* * *

Monday 18/5/42

Sorry I could not finish the letter on Thursday but I had to go into tea. On Sunday we marched the Home Guard up Brooke Hill, and the bugles conked out on the way; but what could you expect we had marched about a mile before we came to the hill and our lips just would not work.

* * *

Friday 22/5/42

The Home Guards demonstrated two Blacker bombards which throw a 20 lb. glorified grenade with fins, for a considerable distance. They were demonstrated on an old car and a projectile went <u>clean through it</u> (it was a dummy and did not explode).

On the same car was demonstrated a Northover projector, which can throw different types of grenade, and hit the car 3 times out of 4.

Lewis guns were also demonstrated and were shown to be very effective.

Then came the Sten gun. This is the sweetest and most desirable weapon I ever set eyes on, for it is a Tommy gun, firing shots singly or like a machine gun, takes standard types of German ammo, and hence is admirable for Paratroops or guerrillas. It takes 32 round clips and will fire about 375 rounds a minute, is effective up to 50 yards, and to crown it all costs only 25/- to manufacture.

You will be pleased to hear that I am now Patrol Leader of the Woodpigeons in the Scouts, and I will try for the Wirelessman's badge shortly.

I have now fixed up an earth through the floorboards of my study. (There will be a fearful row if Mr. Goodchild finds out) and have made my set a two-valve as it did not work with three. In testing however, I unfortunately made a wrong connection (Oh, Woe is me!!!) and blew two valves. My battery has completely expired, and I have to borrow from others if I want to use it.

Thanks awfully for the P.O. you sent, it will save me from becoming penniless in the extreme.

I extend to you the compliments of the season (Whitsun) in receipt of yours.

There is a craze on at the moment for model aeroplanes, but I have abstained partly from lack of funds and partly from lack of enthusiasm.

P.S. Furley & Hassan's won't have any more hats for the duration.

I hope the fruit trees are O.K. It's lovely weather for them. I have managed to work out one of the problems in the penguin book.

I saw an old map in a shop here. It wasn't very expensive, so I sent it to Mum and Dad. It shows Felpham, where we had our holiday with the Edwards' just before the War started.

Saturday 23/05/42

Here is a Whitsun parcel for you which I hope you will like. There is no more news since yesterday. I hope you both have a very happy Whitsun.

P.S. I am now bankrupt.

* * *

Postcard — Sunday 31/5/42

Thank for the P.O. and letter cards, parcel and your letters. Tonight and Yesterday we had the play by G.B.Shaw, "Captain Brassbound's Conversion". It was extremely well acted, and we had a collection in aid of the Red Cross which was quite successful. We started swimming last Sunday but it is very cold. Swimming is compulsory until you have swum your length but as I have swum mine, I will be all right. On Wednesday I bathed again with a thermometer reading of 56° Fahrenheit (water). It was very cold. It's a pity about the fruit but I hope we get a lot of plums and black-currants. I hope you liked the map. It was the only one they had, or I would have got one of more interest to us. Did you notice Folpham (Felpham) and Gr. Bognor (Bognor Regis)? I got it at that shop on the way to the station.

We had a half-day at Whitsun, and I went out for a walk although it drizzled and blew. I liked the parade all right, but it's rather a fag cleaning your uniform. I regret to say that the troop is still slack. I did not think it was worth doing anything about the uniform so I didn't.

* * *

Postcard — Thursday 12/6/42

Thanks for your letter. I think it would be best if you came the Sunday after Speech day, but I enclose the invitation all the same.

I forgot in my last letter to tell you that we had a dog-fight over here. The Jerry got away, but a Spitfire was shot down and the pilot died three days later from a head injury. We had a field day on Tuesday in conjunction with the Corps and had a good time. We are beating retreat on speech day, as will be seen by the invitation. I hope that the blossom is now O.K. (Fruit). I can now swim the side-stroke. No more room.

* * *

Thursday 25/6/42

Sorry I did not write on Sunday, but I went to the matron at the San. and I had not had time during the week.

Thank you for your letters. I am sorry I have caused you so much worry, but there is not much to write about except the "daily round, the common task etc., etc." I am getting on well at swimming now and have invented a kind of sidestroke which I now use always. The half term reports have come out and I came 8th as I did in the first two reports. There are no plays or anything on Speech Day, but there are plays and a "Gut" at the end of the term. I will see if I can come back with a split lip so as to have kept up my record for a year. I am looking forward to seeing you on speech day and hope Dad can come as well. Please let me know what train you are coming on, what meals I am coming out to etc. Please bring some tuck as I am running rather short at present. I am doing a lot of bugling at the moment, practicing for "The Retreat" on speech day.

PS – I have got a new French Violin piece called "La Cinquantine. It is rather nice.

I'm sure they do their best in the Wharflands kitchen, but we all seem to think about food a lot these days. Mum & Dad also seem to be finding that the rations don't go very far — Mum said in a letter that a lot of things that weren't rationed have just disappeared from the shelves in Lipton's.

Monday 29/6/42

Thanks for your letter. I am sorry I was so indefinite in the letter, I meant "I went to tea with matron". I had a jolly good time. We have played a lot of cricket this term and on one game I caught one person and ran two others out. (I was wicket-keeping). I suppose that you mean that you are coming on Saturday, you just said the 12.55. If I meet you I am afraid I will miss dinner, so I think I had better meet you at the Crown at about 1.30 in the Lounge. I hope Dad makes a lot of runs in the A.R.P. match. Please let me know how many he makes.

It is lovely swimming these days, the temperature is now steady at about 70° F. I hope the tomatoes and the other fruit is coming along all right. It's rather a blow about jellies, but I suppose we can't have everything these days.

It was great seeing Mum and Dad at the week end. Dad was talking a lot about what I should do when I leave school. It needs a lot of thought.

Monday 12/7/42

Thanks for the letters, and treatise (I hope I have spelt it correctly). I would like to know more about electrical engineering and forestry please, as I think I would like to take up one of the two. Thank you very much for coming over, I enjoyed the weekend very much. Thanks also for the money. We are all learning our parts of the dorm play frantically and I nearly know my part now. Then I will soon be home again. Abbot's people came over last Saturday and took me out for tea at the Crown and I had a good time.

* * *

Thursday 16/7/42

I went out for a walk to a place called Langham which has a church nearly as big as Oakham. Unluckily I could not explore the village, although I went into the church. I also saw an old house about the age of the San and with ivy on the walls and a lovely garden. I wish you could have seen it. I also saw a modern house (1926) but it was built in the same style, and was made of stone and looked very nice.

On Wednesday we had a swimming parade at scouts. The temperature was only 65° F. but it was alright once you got warmed up. I have perfected my sidestroke now, and can go quite fast.

I have acquired a catapult, and will be able to have some good fun with it on the train coming home.

P.S. I have written to Nana and Auntie Betty.

The Summer holiday will be fun, with a lot of time spent at the ice rink as usual. There's also a plan for me to go and stay in the Lake District with Uncle Walter, Auntie Nancie and my cousin David, who is my own age. We should have a great time. After that there's going to be another rail journey, when Uncle Walter's family take me along with them to visit the rest of our tribe in Ryhope. That's something else to look forward to.

11 Carleton Place
Penrith
Cumberland

Monday 17/8/42

As you see I have now arrived safely in Penrith which has a nice ruined castle (Cromwells artillery reduced it). I had rather a rush at Crewe, but managed to get on the train all right. At Penrith someone ran off with my luggage and did not see the labels. However they have returned it and I am now all set for a nice holiday, I have played Bezique, Monopoly, Main Line, and Sorry with David.

On Friday night I went and watched the swimming at the pool, which is the dammed up Eamon. We went swimming yesterday ourselves, and it was rather cold, but you can go terrifically fast with the current.

Yesterday we also went for a ride to Ullswater which is a lovely lake, surrounded by trees. The Lake steamer was also there, and is a lovely grey oil driven affair. There is some fishing from a boat and they are 2/6 an hour. In the evening we went to Brougham (pron. "Broom") castle where we did some <u>dangerous</u> climbing.

We eventually reached the roof over the gateway, and found where the portcullis had been, and climbed back again. We also went up to the top of the keep. They are feeding me very well and I am having a jolly good time.

P.S. Some day we are going to climb Helvellyn and Saddleback.

* * *

Postcard — Monday 24/8/42

Since I last wrote we have been to see Aira Force and Haweswater dam. Uncle Walter is coming back tonight, and we hope to climb Saddleback tomorrow. Will write on weekend with further details. Hope greengages are ripening.

* * *

11 Carleton Place
Penrith
Cumberland

Tuesday 25/8/42

Thanks for your letter. It's been raining like anything all day today, and we have not been able to do anything, but we are going to the pictures tonight, and will see "Hi Gang". The other day we saw "Blood and Sand", which was very good.

I have written to Ridgeway, Grandpa, and Nana, and I will write to Auntie Alice today to tell her which train I am coming on. I leave on Thursday.

I hope you got the other letter and the postcard.

We went to Haweswater the other day, and saw the dam, which is a magnificent construction of concrete, and will supply Manchester.

Another time David and I went to Aira Force which is very fine, and is not the sort of thing you would like to fall down. Yesterday David and I cycled to Ullswater and along it to Patterdale, and leaving our bikes climbed Helvellyn.

We went along Striding edge, which is about 3 or 4 feet wide, rugged, and has a practically sheer 600 ft. drop on each side, in a thick mist. The top of Helvellyn was also misty.

(On Helvellyn and Striding edge are memorials to people who have fallen off.)

On Helvellyn was a monument to Bert Hinckler who landed a plane there in 1923 and took off again for a stunt.

It took us the whole day.

Uncle Walter arrived safely, and we went for a walk on Sunday.

Uncle Walter was a bit worried when David and I got back late from that cycle ride.

11 Carleton Place

Monday night 24/8/42

Dear Norman and Winnie,

Twice in this last hour or so I have wished you could see that son of yours, and since that is unfortunately not possible, I'd better try my hand at describing him. He and David set off on their bikes at about 11, cycled to Patterdale, climbed Helvellyn by the tough way over Striding Edge, took the wrong path on the top, but found themselves again and returned via Grisedale Tarn.

They arrived home just before 9, when we were beginning to get worried. I had thought they would be thoroughly tired, but not a bit of it – Geoffrey looked as fresh as paint, and gave no sign of anything but an immense hunger. David immediately took off his wet shoes and stockings, and washed his feet, hands and face, but Geoffrey was only prevailed on to remove his stockings with difficulty, and I hadn't the heart to withhold him from his food any longer, so he postponed the washing until later.

Then it was that I wished, for the first time that you could see him – getting round scrambled eggs on toast, with fried potatoes, and then with deep apple pie — then his half pint of milk and cake. He has a rare colour on him, and was as chirpy as a sparrow. Immediately afterwards they retreated to bed, and I have just been up, and wished you could see him again. The two of them are lying on their tummies, with one book between them – one which I specially chose for them at the library this afternoon, called "Wizardarious Happenings" and there they are mopping up the gory details of age old murder mysteries, and what happened to the "Cyclops" and the curse of the Hapsburgs. I have just directed them to a particularly juicy one – "The mystery of the invisible bloodstains."

Tomorrow we plan (if I get up in time) to go to Ullswater, over Place Fell and by Gage Tarn to High Street and then by the Roman Road to Ullswater and to finish by taking the steamer to Pooley Bridge. I have remarked to Geoffrey that is a pity that you are not here, so that the fathers might send the sons ahead as light columns and themselves bring up the rear in a slow and dignified manner.

We all went for a walk last night, and got amongst a big expanse of heather in full bloom – a lovely sight. By the way, have you thought of making G. a politician! He has a great penchant for leaving no stone unturned. He spent some considerable time hurling boulders into a river, and more in heaving still bigger ones over a quarry edge. If he keeps it up he will undoubtedly leave several marks on the face of Britain.

All of which is really to say that he is having a good time, and that we are thoroughly enjoying having him here. It is unfortunate that the weather is still too cold for bathing or for much sitting around, but good for walking.

Nancie is going over for an interview at Carlisle tomorrow with the Appointments Office – they have nothing particular in view, but want to have a look at her and get her registered.

I hope I shall see you soon again on my travels.

Yours

Walter

It was an amazing train ride from one side of the country to the other. Now Uncle Walter is going to walk round with me to my mother's family, the Bowman's, just across the village.

18 Gibson Terrace
Ryhope
Sunderland

Tuesday 8/9/42

Thanks for your letter and the parcel. The plum crop was very nice. We arrived safely in Newcastle, and I went on to Ryhope. I have visited everybody, but Graeme is away on holiday. I have also been helping at the shop. I have also been having some sarsparilla from Mrs Bowles.
You don't say whether you received my first letter (this is my 3rd).
We saw "The Foreman went to France" yesterday. I am coming home on Friday next. I will telegram the times later.
P.S. We had an air raid the other night.

I'm sorry I missed seeing my cousin Graeme, but I did see his sister Jennifer and all the others. The time just flew past and before I knew it I was on the train back to Birmingham again. There were a few days at home — seeing Paula and Mariane and going to the ice rink once more before it was time to catch another train — back to Oakham.

Year Four

Autumn 1942 — Summer 1943

Postcard — 18/9/42

I arrived safely about 3 o'clock. I have got the rugger boots, black jacket, trousers and socks (26 coupons). I am in the Lower 10 Dormitory, and on the next but one to senior table. There are 12 new boys.

Monday 20/9/42

Thanks very much for the money, cake, biscuits etc., which you sent for my birthday.
So far apart from your present I have received

10/- from Nana
10/- fromAuntie Betty
5/- from Auntie Kitty and Uncle Tom
5/- from Grandpa
3/- from Auntie Ethel
3/6 book voucher from Auntie Edith and Uncle Billy
3/- from Auntie Alice and Uncle Cecil.

So I am pretty well off. I bought an accumulator with the money you sent, and am having it charged. My status is now that:-
I am in the senior changing rooms
I am in the back of the house (i.e. I may have two coat buttons undone).
I am now in the upper set of V.
I have moved 1 row further back in chapel.

I have now settled down nicely, and learning the beginnings of co-ordinate geometry.

The cake and anzac biscuit are enjoyed and appraised by all.

I have started as a recruit in No. 10 platoon in the O.T.C. and have learned to march, turn, wheel, about turn on the march, fall in, and open order march. I am enjoying it very much.

The weather here has been good, although it is getting nippy in the mornings.

I will see Furley and Hassans about the striped trousers.

I am taking Science instead of Geography. I hope this will meet with your approval.

Being 14 doesn't feel much older than 13, although it has the advantage of being not an infant any more.

Our housemaster, Mr. Goodchild, nicknamed the Payson, is also the school chaplain. He's actually pretty decent, but he seems to think that everyone else is decent too, even some of the unruly louts that are in Wharflands now. He's taken away some of the Seniors' powers and things are getting very slack.

I'm still persevering with the violin and may join a sort of improvised musical group called The Georgians.

* * *

Sunday 3/10/42

Thank you for your letter. Since last Sunday I have received some money from Penrith. I will have to start on some thank you letters soon.

Rugger has been started although the ground is hard, and your ankles ache afterwards. I managed to score a try the other day, and succeeded in hurting someone's hand to the extent that it is now in a sling.

I have been asked to join the "Georgians" but I have yet to

have a test before I am accepted.

So far this is my happiest term, it is a vast improvement being in the house as the studies are much warmer and less ramshackle.

The house is beginning to go to the dogs. We had 16 new boys this term, and the seniors have practically no power to keep them in order, as it has been all taken by the Payson. By the time I leave, the house will be an utter rabble.

Please excuse the vehemence, but it is a thing we all feel rather strongly about. (For goodness sake don't write or telephone to Mr Goodchild, I'll only get it in the neck).

We had a debate last Saturday on "The motion before the house is that the only satisfactory solution of the German problem is that Germany should be split into small states after the war". It was carried by 51 votes to 37.

P.S. I enclose savings stamps.

* * *

Sunday 24/10/42

I hope you are well. Thanks for your letter. I'm sorry I have not written earlier, but as I am in the School Certificate form I have a colossal amount of prep, and I am often barely able to finish my prep, let alone write letters. On the Sunday before last I went to the Georgians, and had a jolly good time, but although they thought I was good enough, they considered that a violin would be drowned, and they are right in my opinion, as there are two accordians and a drum, making a considerable row.

I am now in the under 14 team and have played in two matches against Stamford and Kingswood. There is a long Sunday on November the 8th. I hope you will be able to come over on that day.

Because the Corps have now got some speech transmitters, I have joined the signals section. We have to send and receive 6 words a minute in morse before we are allowed to use them.

Please send or bring some gloves sometime as it is getting rather cold now.

We had a field day the other week which was rather fun. We had a jolly good time.

Mum and Dad came over for the long week end and stayed at the Crown.

4. Two jacket buttons undone show improved status

Dad is still talking about what I should do when I leave school. But I guess that will have to wait until after the war anyway.

Saturday 28/11/42

Thanks for your letters. I enclose Grandpa's cheque. We have had, as I think I told you when you came over, that there has been an outbreak of measles. A large amount of boys have succumbed, and one boy has had complications, his legs seem to be paralysed, he has to have frequent injections and his feet have had to be hoisted to the ceiling.

We very nearly went home because of the measles, and also because of a second event. Oakham water supply has been running very low, and on the Friday before last there were only 3' of water in the reservoir, and in consequence the water is turned off each night at 8.30. Last Sunday the drums paraded in aid of the Oakham youth movement, and that is why I did not write. The drums and bugles were good, but the fifes were just pathetic and once they fizzled out altogether.

There have been no more under 14 matches because of the measles, but the first XV played Kingswood today, but because some of our best people were down with measles we lost 23 – 0. It was a good game, but about 3 people on each side got wrecked, and 3 people had to be helped off the field.

I am getting on all right in Corps and sometimes have to act as a Lance Corporal, and perform such duties as taking the roll book to the armoury. In the signals we have been learning how to use message books and I have been using a signalling lamp.

I enclose some photos which Lane and I tinted, I am afraid the one of Sidway is rather smudged and the one of Egleton Church is not tinted strongly enough.

I managed to get Dad some 'Passing Clouds' cigarettes for his birthday.

Monday 7/12/42

Dear Dad

Excuse the writing and shortness, but I wrote to wish you many happy returns of the day. I will write more fully when I have time.
I hope you will like the cigarettes, they were the best I could get in Oakham.

Now it's Mum's birthday in a day or two. I'm right out of inspiration, so I think it will have to be another brooch.

Friday 11/12/42

Dear Mum,

Many happy returns of the day. I hope you will like the brooch that I have enclosed.
I am awfully sorry that I will not have time to write more fully, but I have got some prep to do.
I will write as much as I can on Sunday. I am shooting this afternoon, and hope to get a good score.
I have no more time to write now; I hope you will like the present.

Home for the Christmas holidays again. Of course, the parents were out at work all the time and they are very tired too. This is because the Germans have been bombing Birmingham a lot, so the sirens go almost every night and Dad has to do even more ARP duties than usual. When there is an air raid we usually wait until we can hear ack-ack fire before going to our improvised shelter — the cupboard under the stairs. One night there was a loud whoosh but no explosion and in the morning Dad found that a small incendiary bomb had gone straight down one of our drainpipes without exploding. When he got it out it was quite undamaged and I wanted to keep it, but Dad said it must go to the authorities.

In the morning I walked into the centre of the city because the trams had stopped running and it was easy to see why. The whole of New Street and Corporation Street were covered in broken glass and near the Post Office there were fire hoses all across the road.

They managed to get the trams running again by next day, which was just as well, so Mum and Dad could get to work OK. I could also get to the ice rink again — and because Paula and Mariane were on holiday too, I went to the Edwards' quite a few times. On Boxing day there was a super party at a Scout Hall in Kings Heath. A friend of Dad's has two teenage sons who organised everything. There were lots of party games and everyone had brought leftover food from Christmas Day, so we had quite a feast.

Sunday 24/1/43

Thanks very much for your letter. My seniority has improved somewhat. I am now on a higher table, but I am still in the same dorm. I have also moved to a better study.
I had a good journey, and practically finished the "Saint" book. It was awfully hot in the train though.
I am now settling down to school life again.
I have got the tie and black coat, but the only second-hand blazer was the same size as my own. I will see about the pants as soon as possible.
My cough isn't any better, but I sleep in the sick room so as not to disturb the others.
We haven't had any hockey yet, on account of the state of the ground.

The new chaplain, Mr Nynd, is rather a peculiar sort of cove. He says the prayers faster than we do, and as a result we get badly tangled. My study mates are the same as last term.

The train reached Oakham just before 3.

On my table sits a master called Mr Proctor-Robinson. He is a hearty gent and his hobby seems to be making people blush. Everyone bar him has blushed at something he has said.

* * *

Sunday 31/1/43

Thank you very much for your letter.

We played one game of hockey last week. I liked it very much. I was in goal, but in spite of that we won 5 – 3.

I can't really think of much to say, so I will drivel on this and that for a while.

There has been no boxing as yet. The weather is not exactly what one could call perfect, but I have been on a walk in which I unearthed a part of the town of which I had previously been oblivious.

We have looked over some of the Corps wirelesses again, but the essential parts have still not arrived.

My cold is somewhat better. I am seeing about some pants. I am endeavouring to make a crystal set in a matchbox, but whether I shall succeed remains to be seen. Please could you look in the carrier you first presented me with (in cupboard on top of stairs). Therein you will find a crystal, please could you send that over it is about the size of a large pea. It is set in a kind of metal cup.

I am still full of beans etc., but I'm blowed if I can think of anything else to say.

* * *

Sunday 7/2/43

Thanks for your letter and the crystal. I am getting on O.K. with the crystal set. I have bought a morse practice set, so that I can speed my morse up.

We are doing the Pardoner's Tale this term, and are to have a test paper on Monday.

I have arranged to be confirmed, and we have had one or two classes. could you please tell me the date of my baptism?

I am getting on in Corps O.K. I am now no longer a recruit. I will try and see about the coupons, but the fact of the matter is that I did not get an order form from the school to go and get the boots (so that their price is put on the school bill) as is the general practice. This may make the head man rather ratty.

Mr Proctor-Robinson is arranging a house play called "Tobias and the Angel". I may have the small part of Azorah a Circassian dancing girl. (I hence, am half strangled, and beaten with a rawhide whip). I am also organising the lighting. Doing the electrics is fun. The reflectors for the lights are made from Huntley and Palmer's biscuit tins and I have to replace the fuse wire with nails in the fuse box to stop them from blowing all the time. The wiring does get a bit hot, though.

The weather is sunny, but with a cold wind. skates are unobtainable in Oakham.

Dad's got a new job, assistant manager at the New Street branch of the bank. It's a huge building and looks a bit like Birmingham town hall.

Sunday 14/2/43

Thank for your letter. You were right in supposing that the Pardoner's Tale is from Chaucer. It isn't really hard once you get the hang of it. I did fairly well in the test last week.

As to the play I doubt if I will be Azorah. I will most probably be Anna the good hearted, rough tongued wife of Tobit.

I'm afraid that there is no long Sunday this term, so please yourself when you come over.

I'm glad to hear that Dad is settling down O.K. at New Street.

I have got a book called "Radio control for model aircraft" and one called "Pellucidar" by Edgar Rice Burroughs with the book token I took back with me.

There has been more hockey which I enjoyed.

* * *

Sunday 21/2/43

Thank you very much for the parcel and the letter card.

I am writing this in the evening to post it tomorrow as I was taking part in a play rehearsal all this afternoon.

The contents of the parcel were very welcome and delicious. I will try to do some prep before you come over.

You will be pleased to hear that so far this term my nails have been fairly intact.

I have played some more hockey, and for two games have gone into a higher lot, and in the second I managed to get the ball off an army P.T. instructor who was playing.

I am very much interested in the book I got on radio control. There is, so rumour has it, going to be a sing-song in the dining hall tonight, admittance only with musical instrument, I think I will turn up with my violin.

I received the Hallfieldian O.K.

There was a perfectly marvellous sunset the other week, the cloudy sky looking like the inferno of an oil fire.

* * *

Wednesday 3/3/43

I am sorry that I did not write on the weekend but the Masons took me out, and I had a rehearsal to do for the play. I am writing this after I have finished my exam in form, so please excuse the pencil and paper.

The Senior Steeplechase was run last Thursday, and a Wharflands boy was 4th (He smokes like anything). The boy who was 1st was only 59 secs. off the record. I went out with some water and a sponge, and stood about halfway round the course, and ran alongside Wharflands people and sponged their faces. I hope I have laid up treasure in heaven, as the Junior steeplechase is tomorrow.

We went on a field day yesterday, and I have never been so tired in my life. We started about 9.30 and got back at 4.15. During that time I had one mouthful of water; although I had something to eat. When we came back 4 side drums one other bugler and myself marched the Corps around the field. (On the field day itself, I was at the double most of the time). The whole Corps was highly congratulated on its performance by some war office gent.

NB Who is local vicar and local church?

Please could you see if there is any crepe hair, spirit gum and grease paint to be had in Brum at theatrical stores?

P.S. The Theatrical stuff is for the play, very important.

R.S.V.P.

* * *

Sunday 14/3/43

Thank you for your letter. I enclose a list of what make-up is required if you would be so good as to get these things, and, if possible, bring them over for confirmation. A cheque will be handed over when you come over. Mr. Proctor-Robinson is extremely grateful, as there is no make-up in the school.

I ran in the steeplechase (Junior) on Thursday, and came 36th out of 96. I was an utter ruin at the end, but I recovered after tea.

On Saturday there was a running match against the Uppingham 2nd VIII, and our star lost his shoes, and came in about 6th. One of our people however was 2nd.

I went to see the Head man on Friday and he asked me if I had my questions re confirmation. I asked him about re-incarnation, and whether animals had souls etc., etc.

P.S. Crêpe hair is sold in hanks.

5. Oakham's headmaster, G. Talbot-Griffith

Mum came over for the week end and brought the make-up. She had a look at my study at Wharflands, which was not too untidy for a change and also got to meet the Headmaster, Mr. Talbot-Griffith. We call him the Head Man or GTG. He's actually pretty decent but he's got fierce eyebrows and they make him look quite frightening sometimes.

I went with Mum to the Confirmation Service. The weather was rather windy, but we had a good time. She stayed at the Roebuck as usual.

Sunday 28/3/43

Thanks for your letter. I have seen about journey money. I will come on the 9.02 as usual (Thursday) but I will get a single ticket as we do not go back until May 5th.

We had a dress rehearsal of the play last night. We started at 7 p.m. and did not finish till about 11 p.m. although we only did 2 of the 3 acts. We are having the third act this afternoon, and the whole play again tonight.

Last Sunday I went down to communion. I enjoyed it very much. On the way I noticed a large army wireless lorry and van in the yard of the elementary school. After morning chapel I went and got pally with the gents in charge, and eventually they allowed me to transmit (speech) for a while from the lorry. Two other boys spoke to me from the van. It was very exciting.

We had the Elijah on Thursday; it was very good indeed. I drew some of the performers. I will show you when I come home.

I can't think of anything more to say, as I have got to go to the rehearsal.

Another holiday at home. Skating at the ice rink was fun. I really enjoyed it. Food seems a bit short these days. The latest thing is some strange tinned stuff called 'M & V' which stands for meat and vegetable ration. It's just about eatable if you can find an oxo cube to give it a bit of flavour.

Postcard — Wednesday 5/5/43

I arrived safely on time after a pleasant journey. We are beating retreat in the market place on Saturday and there is going to be a pennant presented to somebody or other. There is a semi official <u>rumour</u> that the ceremony will be

broadcasted after being recorded. Please listen if you can.
I am now head of the back of the house.
I will write fully on Sunday.

* * *

Sunday 9/5/43

Thanks for your letter. We paraded yesterday and beat the
retreat in the market place, after the presentation of
Montgomery's pennant to the wife and son of his tank
driver. There was a lot about it in the Sunday paper. There
was no recording. The weather was lousy. 2 hats were blown
off, it rained, and in the end the hands of the fifers were so
numb that they could play no more, and we had to take over
entirely.
We were to have paraded again today but for the fact that the
wind is nearly at gale strength, so there will be no parade.
I have now settled down to work again, but I often feel that
I could do with a skate.
I am happy and well and as I told you in my postcard head
of the back of the house. I will probably be a senior next
term.
I have finished reading "I James Blunt" it is very good. I
think you will like it. Shall I send it home?
I have got the shirts etc.
The tuck cakes, tarts, scones etc., are delish.

* * *

Thursday 20/5/43

I thank you for your sympathetic letters. I was inflicted with
a sore throat with spots in it which is now completely cured.

I am now slightly sunburned (I sunbathed at the san) and back at work. I am in the Finals for the elocution competition. I have had one or two games of cricket, but as I went in last I had no chance to make any runs before the other man was out. I have applied for the refund for my ticket (I temporarily lost it on the train). I will write more fully on Sunday.

* * *

Sunday 23/5/43

Thanks very much for your parcel. The chocolates are lovely.
I went to communion this morning, there were only a few people there.
There will be a field day the Tuesday after next. I will be going out with a wireless.
I am assisting in a small band which is being got up in Wharflands. I am performing on my violin. One boy, who is new this term, is a marvellous pianist; he has won prizes for playing a cinema organ.
The declamation competition finals have not yet been held.
I think the war news at the moment is splendid. We seem to be knocking the stuffing out of the Luftwaffe over Italy.
I forgot to tell you before that my violin bow got battered somewhat in the trunk, and when I tightened it, it broke.
Speech day is July 3rd. We come back on Tuesday July 27th.
We played Ratcliffe School yesterday at cricket, and beat them hollow. They were 122 all out we were 127 for 3 declared.

* * *

Sunday 30/5/43

Thank for your letter. I am very sorry to hear about Mum's bad finger. I hope it is better by now. We have been having very fine weather here, but last night it rained stair rods, brickbats, lions and tigers. We had about 1" or more of rain, it is still drizzling now. It was a dreadful thunderstorm.
We seem to be busy at the moment in giving Italy the "works" from the air.
We had a match yesterday against Wellingborough which we lost. We 120 all out. They 200 for 6 dec. We had the Corps wirelesses out yesterday, and we are taking them out on field day. There is a lot of procedure to learn, but it is good fun.
The swimming baths are not open yet, as the filter has conked out. There are 90 filter cones each with 80 small holes, each of which has to be pricked with a compass point. Only three people can work at a time, as the filter tank is so small.
The declamation prize finals are to be held tomorrow.
Please could you send me "Elmer's tune", "Someone's rocking my dreamboat", "There were two pretty girls", and any other tunes of that ilk you can find in the piano stool or knocking about. Could you also send my ocarina (in my cabinet) as there is someone here who can play it.

Mum sent the music OK. I want it because we're going to have a band to play at a school dance — we are calling ourselves 'The Turning Worms'. It should be a laugh, but McNicol is very good indeed on piano.

Sunday 6/6/43

Thanks for the parcel. I am very sorry to have to report that when it arrived the orange had split, and the cake and patties had crumbled to a powder, and the ocarina was smashed. The remnants are, however, being eagerly devoured.

We had a field day on Tuesday, and I had a lovely time. I did not suffer from thirst as I had filled the flask with water and brought it with me. As arranged, we took out the wirelesses, and helped the defence in the morning. The other post was overwhelmed but they got through a good running commentary of the battle. We were at headquarters. We were eventually mopped up. We had taken the wirelesses about 2½ miles (each wireless weighs 48lbs. exclusive of batteries and earphones and mike). They are carried like a rucksack. We then walked about 3 miles to take up our positions for the afternoon battle. (We again helped the defence). By the aid of the wirelesses we rushed up reinforcements just when they were needed, and the attackers were entirely annihilated, because their main attack was right into a death trap of about 3 Bren guns and a mortar, and we rained bullets on their rear and flank.

The declamation prize was not held last Monday after all, but will be held tomorrow. It is being judged by the headmaster of Uppingham.

Yesterday the XI played Trent and wiped them up. We made 163 runs, and they made 83. Our under fourteen team also won against Kingswood under fourteen. we made 53; they made 27.

There is a big drive going on at the moment for buying prisoner of war parcels. Each parcel contains such things as chocolate, biscuits, cigarettes, tinned milk, minced beef etc., in all costing 10/- made out in 20 6d portions. (One sixpenny ticket will buy the soup or cheese or something). I have raked out 5/- and am pretty well broke.

We had an alert last night before last, but nothing

happened, and I slept right through it.

Swimming started this afternoon, but I did not go in it was only 50°. I hope Mum's finger is better. The weather is lousy.

Mum and Dad hope to come over for Speech Day and stay for the week end.

Thursday 10/6/43

Thanks for your letter and the money. I will enquire at the Crown. I am pleased to hear that your finger is rather better, and that you are having a good time.

I cancel my request in previous communiqué for dough.

I am sorry to say that I did not win the declamation prize. It is an amazing sensation to speak in chapel, the sound echoes back to you.

I am sorry I did not send my letter earlier, but I wanted to enclose my declamation results, and fell ill on Monday. I was violently sick, as were many other boys.

* * *

Sunday 13/6/43

Just a line to let you know that I am still alive.

I enclose the printed card about speech day. I will see if rooms have been reserved at the "Crown" for you.

Tomorrow we get a half holiday, and I will probably go for a walk.

Yesterday the first XI played the town, and it was a draw because of lack of time.

The 2nd XI won against the A.T.C., and the under 14 XI lost by 5 runs against Stamford.

I played cricket on Friday and got 7 runs before being run

out.

Yesterday I went for a swim. It was gorgeous. Myself and our dormitory prefect have formed a belly-flopping society. We take an absolutely terrific run and land flat on the water. It makes a hollow whack and a terrific splash. It is specially to be performed near masters in order to drench them. We are also going to practice stunt ones. (Diving in when I am on his shoulders for instance).

* * *

Sunday 20/6/43

Thank you for your letter and the money.

You will be pleased to hear that I in a rash moment asked to join the choir, and am now a member.

Each platoon has selected a crack section for the section competition. You will be pleased to hear that I am a member of our platoon's section.

I went to tea at Mrs Hill's house to tea last Sunday, and had some lovely little delicacies. I could have told that Mrs Hill was French even if I had not known by those dainty morsels.

On Whit Monday I went to a garden fete at Barleythorpe. It rained intermittently. I joined in a treasure hunt, but did not win. They were selling strawberries and eggs but were sold out before I got my turn. There were numerous side shows, raffles, shove ha'penny etc. I had quite a good time.

I am going to go in for the bronze life saving medallion.

I am glad to hear that Mum's finger is so much better.

You will be pleased to hear that I was 3rd in the half term order.

Sunday 27/6/43

Thank you for your letter. I am very sorry to hear that you may not be able to get over on speech day. It may be possible to get you put up at the "Roebuck" (I believe you said that Mrs Pearce stayed there).

School cert starts on July 9th and takes over a week.

In the two times I have played cricket this week, in one game I made 7 and in another 0.

The Drums are practicing furiously for speech day, and we are also working for the section competition.

I shot for my platoon yesterday, but did not do very well, I am afraid. I adjusted the sights after I had finished, and shot much better. My score was 36 out of 75.

I am managing to master the art of singing tenor. I am enjoying being in the choir.

In the end it was only Mum who could come over for Speech Day, but we had a good time. The Victoria Hall was packed out and it was very hot. I'm looking forward to the summer hols and there's an idea from the Edwards' that I could go on a cycling tour with Paula and Mariane. We'd stay at Youth Hostels and we could get food at British restaurants — they are quite good actually and you can get a hot meal and a pudding for about one and six. Mum will talk to Dad about it and see if they can find me a rucsac.

Sunday 11th July

Thank you for your letter. I'm glad you enjoyed your weekend.

I had my first school cert exam on Friday afternoon. It was a very easy practical chemistry paper. According to my calculations by comparison with the answers of others, I ought to have got somewhere between 60 and 80%.

All this week everyone has been working hard; the main exams start tomorrow.

On Friday, I received a letter from Paula to wish me luck in school cert. I thought that it was very nice of her.

This afternoon we had the junior tests for the swimming sports. It was icy cold. I went in for the two lengths breast stroke, and the two lengths free style but failed to get into the sports as usual.

We had a route march on Wednesday. The Drums headed the column, and we marched to Langham and back. The playing of the Drums was pretty dreadful. I think it was a relapse after speech day. Four out of six side-drums skins went through because of a shower which softened them.

I am to play Handel's Largo in a concert on the last Sunday of term at a concert. I hope I will manage O.K.

The "Wharflands Turning Worms" (that's the band which I joined) had a dance last night which lasted from 8.20 to 10.30. It was a terrific success. The headmaster and his wife, two nurses from Burley (who were extremely popular) Miss Chevalier, and Proctor-Robinson were there as well as many others. The band was got up in three days of practicing during which my playing improved immensely.

* * *

Sunday 18/7/43

Thank for your letter. I went to Illesley's to enquire about the rucsac but was told that it was not a rucsac but a holdall. They have no rucsacs. The price of the holdall is 35/-. There is another saddlers called Craggs which I will try.

You will be pleased to hear that I shot yesterday, for my Empire test, and became a first class shot. I am now entitled to wear a rifle and star on my arm.

Please do not forget to have my bike repaired.

I will probably catch the 7.09 am. train from Oakham, and I will find out later what time I arrive, and inform you.

Please if you are able to meet me bring my skates if you are not thinking of doing anything special.

I have come to the conclusion that the School Certificate is a cinch. The papers so far, even those which I have not looked forward to have been ludicrously easy. Our exams did not finish on the Friday. We have until next Friday to go yet (9 more exams). I have worked out that so far I have written in the 'cert nearly 100 sides of foolscap and 25,000 words.

I'm glad that we are able to go to Corris. What week are we going?

P.S. We had a boiling hot day yesterday. Shall I get journey money here?

* * *

Wednesday 21/7/43

I am just dropping you a line to let you know what train I am catching. I will catch the 7.09 a.m. train from Oakham. I change at Leicester and arrive at Birmingham about 10.a.m. (Tuesday)

This enquiry office is nuts. I do not know what time I get in at Leicester nor what time the connection leaves. Can you inform me? Our last exam finishes at 11. a.m. tomorrow, after which I will do no work whatsoever whichever.

Please see if you can meet me with my skates, or have them at New Street. with the key. It is, I believe, in my blue sports coat right hand side pocket. (Unless that is you have made other arrangements for the morning).

All this week we have had tea and bread and jam in Matron's room (the people taking Cert. only) the others are very jealous.

It's great to be home again and go to the ice rink. I really miss skating during term time. The plan to go Youth Hostelling with Paula and Mariane has been sorted out. We will leave in a couple of days.

Clent

Thursday 12th August

I am having a gorgeous time. We set off from the flats at about 3, and went down the Pershore road, until we got to Cotteridge, after which we got lost, and eventually arrived on the Hagley Road. We cycled up and down many hills and eventually arrived here after doing 15 miles. The hostel is a wooden sort of shack erection but is very comfortable. We have two meals, one of bread and marmalade and cocoa and the other of fried bread and tomato. I am really enjoying myself.

The bunks in the dormitories weren't too bad, though there wasn't much room. The girls said theirs were OK too. The only bad thing was having to help with washing up after the meals. Next day we went on to Bridges, near the Long Mynd and finally to Wilderhope Manor, a big old house with the most amazing spiral staircase. We did get a bit lost once (my fault) and Paula had a grumbling appendix, which slowed her down a bit, but we had a great time. Auntie Linda gave us some delicious soup when we got back.

At the end of August we went to Corris in mid-Wales for a few days. We stayed at an amazing pub called the Braîch Goch. The man who ran it had been a chef on the 'Empress of Britain' and the food was fantastic. It seemed that food rationing just didn't happen there, so we ate like kings — sometimes we couldn't finish it all! The other great thing was the chance to ride on the footplate of a steam locomotive. It's on a narrow gauge railway that brings slate to Machynlleth from the quarries near Corris.

Year Five

Autumn 1943 — Summer 1944

Wednesday 22/9/43

I arrived safely at Oakham at about 3, and returned the trousers to Furley and Hassan's. I am now a senior, thank goodness, and am having a wizard time. I have gone into VI and have just settled down. I have given the Headmaster the letter about the coupons, but nothing has happened yet. I will write more fully when I have time.

* * *

Sunday 26/9/43

Thank you very much for the parcel. I am enjoying the contents very much. As you know I am now a senior, a most exalted position, and well worth waiting for. I am permitted full use of the top of the hut, the passage in the house, and am entitled to sing, whistle, put my hands in my pockets etc., etc.

I have received birthday cards from Auntie Edith and Uncle Bill and The Edwards and 10s and a birthday card from Uncle Tom and Auntie Kitty and Grandpa. Could you supply me with their addresses.

I have had two games of rugger which I enjoyed. In the first I got a split lip, in the second someone stood on my hand in the scrum and it bled profusely.

The signals have exchanged our number 8 sets for number 18's which are brand new and more efficient. We have also got a 10 line exchange, six Don-5 telephone sets and 4½ miles of wire.

I am settling down to work, which as yet I don't find too hard.

I enclose my school cert marks. Have you seen any skates my size yet?

Do you wish me to see about extra clothing coupons, or will you do so? I will see about the Cambridge slippers. The band is getting under weigh again; we have now a clarinet.

P.S. Do you think I could have one of the lads over for a week in the holidays?

* * *

Sunday, 3 Oct. 43

Thank you very much for the long letter (and the 10/- from Auntie Pat).

I recovered from the minor rugger injuries, but wrecked my ankle but am now nearly O.K. again. Yesterday we played an old boys XV. They won 21 – 13 after one man had retired with a sprained knee and another had been knocked out and winded, and carried off snoring! I have got a new pen, but I am using this one because I wrecked the new one by screwing the top on, and wrecking the nib which was too long. I have taken it back to the shop.

The corps has now 4 number 18 wireless sets. We are going to use them on a field day. I am going to try for my signaller's badge this term.

I have managed to get some apples. They are quite nice.

You will be pleased to hear that I am now second bugler, and have managed to obtain a battledress.

I am still sharing a study with Wilson and Whitlock.

The Wharflands play is either going to be "The Moon is Down" or "Thunder Rock".

P.S. I am thinking of having Mason over in the holidays. O.K.?

* * *

Monday, 10th Oct. 43

Thank you very much for the parcel. I like the sweater very much. The pears were lovely.

I apologise for writing in pencil, but my old pen's nib smashed yesterday night. I also apologise for not answering your questions, but I was in rather a hurry, and failed to remember.

Please see about the skates at your earliest convenience. They will be (probably) more expensive towards Christmas (If you have to spend any more money, I will send it if you let me know). It would be best to phone an application the same night as that on which the advert appears in the Birmingham Mail.

Furley and Hassan's have only one double breasted dark grey coat, and that did not fit me. What shall I do?

Davis' have only one pair of Cambridge slippers (too small), but they have some leather ones (14/6). Shall I get a pair of those?

The corps has received 4 more wirelesses. We now have 8 — 4 number 18 sets (range 5 miles, weight 30 lbs) and the most recent type of set, 4 number 38 sets (range 3 miles, weight 10lbs). There is now 1 wireless set for each member of the signals. We are going to have a fine time on field day.

I went to the pictures yesterday, but owing to the fact that the posters were rather vague, I did not know what I was going to see. It was a western, an abomination called "The Masked Rider", everyone was shouting "Look behind you", etc. etc. to the hero when he was about to be shot at by the villain, but I enjoyed the film all the same.

Our 1st XV played Uppingham 2nd XV yesterday, we were beaten 31 – 0

P.S. I am taking my Adexolin and Vitamin C tablets.

Food seems to be a bit short this term, but we had macaroni cheese one day and I managed to get a second helping — and some tomato sauce!

Sunday 17/10/43

Thanks for your letter. I am very pleased to hear that you have managed to get some skates. I am absolutely dying to do skating again.

I am taking the first part of Certificate 'A' on Tuesday. I hope I will get on all right.

I would like to see the Chrysanthemums. How big are they? It rained all night, and it is very wet underfoot.

All the leaves of the trees in Church Street have fallen, and they look very cold and bare.

On Wednesday afternoon in rugger a nail in my rugger boot penetrated my foot. I went down to the San the following morning and after having it dressed I had an Anti-Tetanus and Septicemia injection just in case I got blood poisoning. I am now quite O.K.

Yesterday I laboured for two hours woodcutting which didn't seem to be funny to me.

I am now a P.T. instructor. (We do PT for 15 mins. after morning lessons). It is rather fun, but owing to the fact that I strive to be efficient, my study mate (Wilson) who is a member of the form which I take becomes mildly annoyed, and swears at me afterwards.

I am sorry to hear of Dad's boil, I hope it is better by now.

* * *

Sunday 24th October 1943

Thank you very much indeed for the parcel, I am enjoying the contents very much.

I regret to say that I made a mistake as to the date of cert. 'A'. It is next Tuesday.

For part I of Cert. 'A' the syllabus is:-

Physical Tests:

5 mile march in 1 hour 10 mins. (I completed this with quarter of an hour to spare. I was first.)

100 yards in 10 secs.   )
3 heaves on a beam, (get chin over top)) I did not do these
15 feet climb on a rope   ) because of my
5 feet standing jump   ) wrecked ankle.
4 feet vault or high jump   )
1 mile in 6 mins. 20 secs.   )

Foot and Arms Drill

Care, cleaning, loading, aiming, and knowledge of the parts of a rifle.

Map Reading:-

Map references, symbols and co-ordinates.

Tactics:- command a section in an assault on a light machine gun post.

When you come over I would certainly appreciate a jar of jam and some tomato chutney. Please bring the Wireless, and if you can bring 1 or both of the skating boots. I would like to see them and try them on. Please bring some winter underwear with you, my Aertex is slowly but surely disintegrating.

I have started on my thank you letters, and have got my hair cut.

The signals have received some records on correct speech and use of the wireless sets.

Lane (head bugler) and I are absolutely overwhelmed with bugle recruits, ten in number, out of which we are to select two for the Drums. They are all as keen as mustard, and are practicing continually at all hours of the day.

I wonder if you could so your famous string pulling act to get hold of a copy of "Thunder Rock" and also "The Moon is Down" in play form for Mr Proctor-Robinson.

Could you please see if you can get me a book on skating, or if not get hold of a title, and I could order it here.

I have got hold of a very good idea for when I leave here from one of the boys. Go to Faraday House in London (a kind of mechanical and electrical academy). After two years I take a BSc. and go on to a factory on a four-year course (at the factory you pass from department to department and earn £4 a week). You then, I believe become an M.I.E.E. could you get details of this please?

P.S. The tomatoes did not spread over the parcel.

I wrote two poems this week, and here is one of them:

TO AN OLD COAT OF ARMS FOUND IN A VILLAGE CHURCH
Thou oaken plaque
On thee a craftsman lavished priceless skill
Thou standest still
Where hand of long dead knight had placed thee
The years defaced thee
Thou wert while kings did fall
The emblem of a knight, his life, his all.

I got a parcel with a long interesting letter from Dad.

27th October 1943

Dear Geoffrey,

We were very pleased to have your letter and Mum will be writing later.

Enclosed are your winter 'undies', a new pair of house shoes and a book on skating.

We were very pleased with your result in the Five Mile March, but think you were wrong when you suggest that you have to run the 100 yards in 10 seconds. Probably not a hundred people in the world could do this. Perhaps you mean 12 seconds.

The rest of the tests appear very interesting.

I have tried to buy copies of "Thunder Rock" and "The Moon is Down", but so far without success. I hope to get a copy of "Thunder Rock", but "The Moon is Down" has not, I understand, been published in play form in this country. There was a radio version, but whether this would be any good I don't know.

I am very pleased that you found the Faraday House idea for yourself, because it is one which I had intended to mention to you for some time. You probably have forgotten that "Uncle" George was the Gold Medallist at Faraday House in his year, and I have had a chat with him about the course which suggests that it should be very interesting and a good stepping-stone to a career. the course is roughly as follows:

Year 1.   *At Faraday House. Maths. Physics etc.*
Year 2.   *Is spent at a <u>general</u> engineering factory.*
Year 3.   *At Faraday House. the Diploma year.*

The Faraday House Diploma is an exempting exam for A.M.I.E.E., but the Degree is not awarded until the recipient has spent two years in a responsible position — commerce or local government.

Year 4.   *This is spent at an electrical engineering works and at the end of this it is possible to take the eternal B.Sc. Degree of*

London University.

It is possible that if you can take Higher Certificate in the right subjects this will provide exemption for the Inter B.Sc. perhaps you will make enquiries about this and get yourself put into the right curriculum, if you decide that the Faraday House plan is a good one. I am personally all in favour, although I think it is possible that your mother would like you to go to a university. I think life in London would be just as good and you would be working in something " down your own street".

I like your poem. Try to keep up this side of your activities, because there is nothing so dull as a scientist who is nothing else.

Love from Dad.

I was really pleased to have that, but it all needs thinking about. Mum wrote too, and sent "Thunder Rock".

Monday 1/11/43

Thank you very much for your parcels and letters. I like the book on skating very much. Mr Proctor-Robinson is very pleased with "Thunder Rock" and casting has begun. I am getting one of the biggest parts.

Please <u>don't</u> bring the wireless. I have had one argument with the Head and he seemed to take a poor view. I was going to try again but he became ill and went to bed, so I didn't.

On Wednesday night the boiler blew up and there was a fire in the boiler house. Since then there has been no hot water, but we hope there will be one installed by Tuesday.

I regret to say that there was no Cert. 'A' on Tuesday except for part 2 (more advanced) candidates. part I will be held next term. false alarm!

<u>Tuesday</u>

We were going to have a field day today, but it has been put off till next Tuesday.
In shooting I took my "King George V" Test on Wednesday.
I am looking forward to seeing you on Saturday. What time are you arriving?
I have so far written only two thank you letters. I don't seem to get much time.

Mum and Dad came for the week end and we talked a lot about Faraday House, and I will find out about the curriculum for Higher Certificate. Only a few days after their visit, though, a lot of boys started to get ill. Within another week or so, there was a terrible situation here. The Head Man went down with an outbreak of boils and carbuncles and now everybody seems to be ill. I've been packed off to the San with shingles and there are epidemics raging through the school. There's been lots of flu and 'strep' throats and matron tells me they've got cases of chicken pox, jaundice, scarlet fever and diphtheria too. There are lots of staff ill as well and they had to get V.A.D. nurses from the Red Cross Auxiliary Hospital at Burley-on-the-Hill to help out. At the end of November, there were over 100 boys sick, so it was decided to shut the school until after Christmas. I blame the food.

I had to stay for ages after anyone else, because of the shingles. In the end I was allowed to travel home in the middle of December, when I wasn't infectious any more — though the spots round my middle still itched a lot.

At least I wasn't ill for Christmas, but it all seemed a bit dull this year, as Mum & Dad were so very tired. But they perked up a bit for the Boxing Day party in King's Heath. It was just like last year only there didn't seem to be so much to eat this time. I played cards a lot with Paula & Mariane and went to the ice rink about twice a week, so the end of the holidays came all too soon.

Sunday 23rd Jan. '44

I arrived at Oakham at about 3, and slouched around to Wharflands, and after depositing my goods and chattels, I went and had tea at Barton's with Dudley.

At the moment I hold a rather vague position in the house. No new prefects have been made so there are only three (Beecroft, Dilks and Frisby) but Lane and Myself are dormitory seniors (we call ourselves monitors). Later on we may be made full prefects. I am in the cottage which is very cold upstairs but it is warm in bed, as we have an extra blanket.

Yesterday we had chapel at 11.10 and a pep talk by the Head Man. (To urge us to make an effort to make up for the work lost last term) We then went to our form masters for ¼ of an hour in which we were told what our timetables were, and after that we had a congregational practice. There are only 3 tenors now and one of them (not me!) does not sing tenor at all.

In the afternoon we marched round changing studies, and Lane arrived with a cornet (playable but not edible). I went to see a very poor exhibition of pictures in the Victoria Hall. We had morning service as usual, and I went for a walk in the direction of Ashwell. I have no further news except that I am in the study next door to the one that I occupied last term, and am sharing with Bowman.

Please could you send me an alarm clock if possible, because we are out of range of Bells in the cottage.

Actually, the cottage is rather horrible. There is a bathroom, but the hot water comes from a terrible gas geyser, which goes off like a bomb when you try to light it — and by the time it's produced enough water for a bath, the water already in the bath is stone cold. I left my pants and vest on a chair one night and they were stiff with ice next morning,

so now we all put our vests, pants, shirts and socks underneath our top blankets. That way we can get dressed
without freezing to death.

* * *

Sunday 30th Jan. '44

Thank you very much indeed for the parcel with prunes,
(am just eating the last one) and the letter-card.
Last Monday I had my first game of rugger, and it was the
worst I have every played in. It poured with rain and an icy
wind blew (I found my rugger boots yesterday, but up to
then I was playing in a pair which did not belong to anyone.
I will keep them just in case). I played in another game on
Tuesday and scored a try. I enjoyed this game rather more.
On Saturday we had a lovely game and I was complimented
on my tackling ability by the master who took us. (I played
inside three-quarter in this game).
On Tuesday we had Corps, and we were issued with the
new webbing equipment. The brass work does not have to
be cleaned, and there is a subtle sort of buckle at the front.
We had a morse-practice signals parade afterwards.
On Friday I did some physical efficiency tests for Cert. 'A'
and got all of them. they were:-

100 yards in 13 secs
4ft 3" vault or jump
6ft 6" standing long jump
Climb 24ft of rope and slide down again
Heave to chest and without touching floor
Heave again to knees.
As a result of these I am a physical wreck, and I can't move
a muscle without twingeing somewhere.

I laboured on Thursday, and shovelled the best part of 2 tons of anthracite. This did not help my physical condition much. We had our first "Messiah" practice on Monday night. I like it, but it is rather difficult.

It has now turned out that I have badly pulled some stomach muscles, and I'm off games, labour etc., all this week.

On Saturday morning the corner of the playing field was occupied by a Royal Artillery detachment. They set up a Bofors Ack-Ack gun and aimed it at nearly all the planes that come over. They were only on manoeuvres however, and cleared off early on Monday.

My new study mate is O.K. he lives at Grantham.

I don't think I shall be wanting my Meccano set any more. I asked Dad to try and sell it through the small ads in the Birmingham Mail. I've got a watch now — the Edwards' managed to get it thorough some contact with the American forces.

We had a bit of a drama in the cottage, where we have a downstairs study with an open coal fire. One of my stupid study mates had a can of 'Meat Soup' (you never know what sort of meat!). He put it on the fire to heat up and then forgot. There was an explosion! Nobody hurt, but it took ages to clear up the mess — and the soup was burnt too.

Sunday, 6th Feb. 1944

Thank you very much indeed for your share in the procuring and buying of the watch. It has been the subject of great admiration from the Head Man downwards. It's OK by me to pay £5 towards it.

About Meccano. there are 750 parts, an electric motor and transformer with a speed controller. But before you advertise ask the Edwards if the people they know want it. Don't bother about an alarm clock. I think I will be able to manage without one. the cottage is very warm downstairs, but its freezing upstairs.

My stomach muscles have healed up remarkably quickly and I am now perfectly OK. I will see about 'Thunder Rock'. I believe Mr Watts has got it.

The biscuit tin is safe and sound in my study. I don't think anything is being done about the play.

There isn't really any news as I have been off games and Corps all this week.

Yesterday and today it has frosted hard, and there is a bit of ice on the static water tanks. If there are any more frosts, I may be able to do some skating.

Please could you send me a tablecloth. At the moment we don't possess one.

P.S. You can sell the Meccano to the "best offerer". The watch keeps excellent time. Thank you once again.

Dad has come up with another idea for me. He's found out that there are engineering degree courses at King's College Cambridge and wants me to ask the School what they know about them.

Wednesday 17/2/44

Thank you very much indeed for your letter. I am sorry I did not write during the weekend, but I will tell you all about that later.

I had a letter from Paula last week. (Monday night, I think). We have had a bit of snow here. On Saturday morning there was a sprinkling on the ground, and also on Monday and Tuesday, but it has all melted now, and the sun is shining with all its might, so it doesn't look as if there will be any skating after all.

I have never seen so many troop carriers (hush!!) as there are round here now. The sky is absolutely black with them (American 'Dakotas')

On Monday (last week) we played a junior house match (second lot and downwards) against school house. We won 16 – 0!!!!

On Thursday we played a senior house match with School House using the best men we could muster. I dashed down to Furley and Hassans and found that they had 10 Wharflands rosettes, 3 of them had long trailing ribbons. I bought the lot at 6d each and I went back to Wharflands, and selecting the best 'tailed' one for myself announced the fact that I had nine for sale. I was instantly pounced on by a mob, and was lucky to get away with my life. I did (needless to say) a roaring trade. I managed to borrow two megaphones out of the armoury. I also found a klaxon horn, and I led the cheering on the touch line armed with my megaphone and rosette, ably supported by 9 lusty rosette wearers and many others, among whom the remaining klaxon and megaphone had been distributed. Never in my life have I seen such a tough game. Everyone on each side was on the top of his form, and although they had the heavier scrum and the ball was within 25 yards of our line for the vast majority of the game, they only won 3 0, which was very good considering their superior age and might.

We played a junior match against the Day Boys in which I played (second row in the scrum). They put up a tough resistance in the first half, and we only got one try in that half. But we got five more in the second, making the final score 18 – 0.

Mrs Griffith has just had a baby daughter and we had a half day today to celebrate. There is a school collection being made for a christening present.

Thursday

I will now explain (with profuse apologies) why I did not

write during the weekend. Last week I wrote and re-wrote a story that I had thought of on the Sunday night Mum was here. I borrowed a typewriter from one of the masters, and laboriously typed it out. This unfortunately took me the whole of the weekend, and I was unable to write a letter. I sent my typewritten copy together with a letter to Pocket Publications Ltd. (Lilliput), and have not yet received an answer so they evidently have not chucked it out straight away. (I enclosed stamped addressed envelope for return of the M.S. in case they did not like the story.)

I would like to have been at the social at St Hughes and to have heard Mr Daw sing his soul searing, heart rending ballad.

I will enquire about the course at Kings College, Cambridge.

I will not post this letter till tomorrow morning to see if a reply from Lilliput comes by the morning post.

P.S. No letter from Lilliput yet.

* * *

Wednesday 1/3/44

Thank you for your letter and the parcel. I have finished the raisins, and I have nearly finished the prunes. I will try to be tidy when you arrive on Saturday.

Nothing much has happened since I last wrote, except that we have about 1½ inches of snow on Sunday, traces of which still remain. We had one or two good snow fights.

There is still no word from the Lilliput people. I think they must have thrown my story away. I have, however, an idea for another one.

When you come over, please could you bring my wireless (surreptitiously, of course). The voltage in the cottage is 230, and I can run it quite safely in there without the Head Man finding out.

Two of the corps wirelesses have gone west, but we took them to pieces and found out what was wrong, and we have sent up for the spare parts.

Mum and Dad brought the radio. It works just fine in the cottage. I can even get the American Forces Network, so we're up to date with the latest Glenn Miller and Tommy Dorsey numbers!

Sunday 12/3/44

Thank you for your letter. The weather here is unsettled but the snow has entirely disappeared, and the weather tends to be warmer.

On Monday I played off my fives competition, there were three games. The scores were 15 – 11 (won) 15 – 7 (lost) 15 – 0 (lost). The last game was really dreadful. My partner did not seem to be able to do anything (Not that I was much good anyway). The two people who went up from our lot were Tozer II (School house) and Sutton (Wharflands). We may win the competition yet.

On Tuesday we did Corps as usual. This time we had practical lessons in field craft from an N.C.O. from a camp near Nottingham.

On Wednesday nowt in particular happened that I can remember.

On Thursday we had a field day. Wright and I operated an 18 together all day. After first period in the morning, we collected the set, and with Sgts. Palmer and Cruikshank (who was in charge of the defence) set out for H.Q. We luckily got a lift in an American lorry however, which took us most nearly all the way there. We walked right round the most westerly wood on our arrival, and decided on the hut for H.Q. We thought an attack from either triangle wood to the northwest or the easterly wood likely, so strong forces were posted in the north of the wood. We set up our wireless in the hut, and stood the aerial out of the door. The set was on a table, and the operator had a box with a <u>cushion</u> to sit on. An ordnance survey map draped on the wall completed the furniture, and it would have done credit to the B.B.C. Soon after our arrival, Tozer arrived with a 38 set, and went out on several recce patrols, and got us a running commentary of the battle.

The first attack was from triangle wood, which consisted of a two section attack. The ground was favourable for the attackers, and Stanton's section had to be rushed up to stem the advance. The two attacking sections were captured together with considerable booty. About 90 rounds of "ammo" and a 38 set were captured. Wright took this 38 and he and Tozer went in different directions on patrol. Soon from Tozer, who had gone out to the haystacks, a hurried S.O.S. came up. A platoon was attacking down the track and there was only one bren to stem the advance. I sent a runner and Stanton's section was hastily recalled from the N.W. corner of the wood, and Jacob's section also moved up. The attackers were then met by a murderous cross fire, and the whole platoon was annihilated. Much booty was taken including anther 38. (The platoon in that attack and the two sections in the other attack were judged wiped out by Captain Cox who was acting as umpire). Jacob's section returned to its post, and an S.O.S. was then received from it. Another section was attacking. Sgts. Cruikshank and Palmer took sten guns and joined this section. Soon the attackers were totally wiped out, and two no. 18 sets were captured. We then clocked off for lunch, and another platoon arrived too late to attack anything!

In the afternoon we attacked a small spinney, and nothing

eventful happened, except that the opposing wirelesses strayed onto our frequency, and disclosed their position to us. Wright and myself got a lift at Ashwell cross roads and sailed triumphantly past all the platoon who were footslogging home. Were they sore or were they sore!

On Friday nothing of importance happened.

On Saturday there was a steeplechase against Stamford, which we won by 71 points to 64. Four wireless sets were sent out and spaced round the course. I had the one at the start and finish. Everyone said my commentary was really professional.

Holyoake went to Leicester yesterday to have his ears seen to. He is back again now.

I have got several vague ideas for a story, but I have not had time to write them yet. I have had a letter from Mariane.

I got German Measles, so I was shunted off to the San.

* * *

Sunday 19/3/44

Thank you for your letter. I am now restored to perfect health. I came out of the San on Friday evening.

On Tuesday and Saturday nights we had alerts, and heard planes, but there were no bombs dropped.

On Wednesday, General Montgomery visited Oakham, and a lot of boys saw him. (I unfortunately was in the San).

On Thursday the King came to Oakham but I could not see him either, worse luck. I didn't want to go on the prowl at night to the royal coach because I thought I might give the King German Measles.

On Tuesday the senior steeplechase was run. A School House boy won.

On Thursday the junior steeplechase (in which I would have

run) was run. A Day Boy won.

On Friday afternoon I walked to Braunston to investigate the village. It is very picturesque, and possesses what I believe to be the two biggest Yew trees in England. One of the 2 pubs was open (The Old Plough) and I found that they catered for up to 108 teas on Sundays. We will have to go there in the summer.

Yesterday was confirmation day, and we missed two lessons in the morning. Holyoake was confirmed, and his people came over for the weekend and asked me out for lunch and tea. I think it was very nice of them. They suggested that at the end of term I got the 7.09 a.m. train, had breakfast with them, and made sure of getting the connection (the 10.15 at Leicester).

* * *

Sunday 26/3/44

Thank you very much for your letter. This will be my last letter of the term. The term has flown! I think it's the quickest I have had.

Today it is just like a summer day, and it is really very hot for the time of year. I think we are going to have a serious drought.

Caroline was christened today, the Bishop of Peterborough coming over for the ceremony.

Mrs Hill was ill on Tuesday, so I did not go for a music lesson. She is OK. now.

On Tuesday we had a cert 'A'. I passed with flying colours. (Although I says it as who shouldn't of.)

I had a great time during the Easter holiday but got a nasty boil on my neck and had to have it lanced.

It was extra good at the ice rink and I went there a lot. Dad is getting very anxious about what I should do when I leave school. There will be military service, of course, but perhaps the war will be over. Now that the Americans have joined in, it might finish sooner. Anyway, he's starting to ask around his friends. There's always the Faraday House possibility, but I'm not sure whether electrical engineering is right for me.

Sunday 7/5/44

I arrived here quite safely at about 8 and proceeded to Wharflands, where I now have a study at the front of the house. On arrival I was summoned to the Head Man, and after a lecture on discipline etc., I was duly proclaimed a prefect (Subdued cheers and cries of 'Shame', 'where's that halo?' etc. etc.) After supper the Head Man asked me to think over whether I would like to be a swimming prefect or not. I think I will be one.
(No cricket, No Labour, Much Swimming, Much Sunbathing)
I now have two poor defenceless fags at my beck and call, but I have not started ill-treating them yet!
I am in charge of the Lower 12 dormitory. I haven't had any trouble yet.
Yesterday we had beginning of term service in chapel with the usual pep talk afterwards. Then we did some Dynamics. In the afternoon I went out for a walk along the Braunston road.
How is Dad getting on? I hope he is better by now.
P.S. I don't think I'll be able to get my jacket cleaned. The Yanks have monopolised the cleaners. How is my watch?

* * *

Monday May 15th '44

Here is my state scholarship entry form. Please look it over and do any signing etc., required.

We had declamation semi finals today. I came 3rd out of the whole of the sixth, but only 2 were required for the finals so I didn't get in. Two boys out of our Science form VI_3 are in the final to the everlasting disgrace of the Arts forms VI_1 and VI_2. (Haw! Haw!)

P.S. Send the form back as quickly as possible.

* * *

Sunday 14th May '44

Thanks for your letters. The "boil" has vanished except for a painless bump, and I am still keeping elastoplast on it.

I accepted the post of swimming prefect, and have cut acres of grass with shears at the edge of the baths. I have stripped to the waist each time, and by the end of term I ought to be pretty brown.

My fags are doing quite nicely so far; there has been no cause for complaint. I have, however, slippered one person twice for making a nuisance of himself in the dorm. (Talking after being told to shut up etc.) And I beat two people for being out of bed. (I didn't lay it on at all hard).

We have had 3 eggs per head so far this term. Pretty good isn't it. I am now classed as a section leader. I instruct 'W' section of No. 1 platoon of the Headquarters Company. I instruct people in the use, procedure for use with, how to talk into, the whole 'gen' on the Transmitter, Infantry Number 18, Mark III, and the Transmitter, Infantry, Number 18 Mark IV.

I am glad to hear that Dad is better. I hope he has now

completely recovered.

You will be pleased to hear that I now have 9 finger nails in a perfect state of presentation. The Right hand thumb nail is the only defaulter, and I sincerely hope that it will soon stop defaulting.

I went to the pictures yesterday, and saw a putrid western. There was "I Married a Witch" at the other place but it wasn't showing a matinee.

The weather her has been glorious, but a north wind is blowing at the moment although the sun is shining.

We played the town at cricket yesterday but we were all out for 13!!! Shocking!!

We had a house photo taken in front of Wharflands and I've had the most fantastic week with wonderful weather.

6. The Wharflands house photograph, May 1944

* * *

Sunday May 21 '44

Thank you for the letter and the telegram. I have filled in what remained of the state scholarship form, and it has been sent up. I put down Clare College. Mr Cox has been to Cambridge, and he says that Clare College is good for engineering. (King Peter of Yugoslavia went there).

We played Trent at cricket yesterday (away). We got 121 all out and they got 158 for 5 declared. The 2nd XI also played the A.T.C. We got 108 for 3 wickets declared and they got 146 all out.

I have been doing a good lot of work at the baths lately; I worked a suction pump to suck slime off the bottom all Thursday afternoon.

7. Manning the pump at the swimming baths

I will probably do some painting there next week. Swimming has not started yet. We are still waiting for the temperature to go up. The baths are pretty well ready.

I have been to Furley and Hassan's and settled with them about the blazer (I got one) the trousers and a jacket. I think they are writing to you.

I shot my Empire Test again on Saturday. I got 1st class again, scoring 66 points out of 80 against 54 out of 80 last time.

I am still instructing people in the art of using the 18 set, but most of the work is done for me by ready-made lectures by Alvar Liddell on gramophone records.

I have heard that 5 members of the staff are leaving next term. I am not sure who they are.

Last Sunday I had tea with the Matron at the San. It was a lovely tea.

Are the Culls or anyone staying with you at Stratford? I hope the weather is OK for you. It has been rather cold and drizzly here lately.

P.S. Monday – I got your letter this morning. Glad to hear the food is good. I will have to visit your hotel at Stratford-on-Avon. The weather is fine this morning. I hope it is for you. You ought to row on the river.

* * *

Sunday 28th May 1944

Thank you very much for the parcel and the card. I have demolished the pork pies as per instruction. They were delicious. I haven't tried the cake yet, but the buns are very nice, especially the ginger ones.

I am glad to hear you have been having such a good time. If the hotel is good enough for me it must be a good one, because from now on I judge them all by the Braîch Goch at Corris.

The baths are nearly ready now. We have got all the muck off the bottom, and the water is as clear as crystal. We were fitting up the chlorinating plant the last time I went, so the chlorine is probably going in now. I am just beginning to learn the intricacies of the filtering and pumping plant.

On Friday I took the most junior set for cricket (very small boys) owing to the illness of the person who generally takes them. They behaved quite well.

There is to be a beating of the Retreat on Speech Day, but I should not think it will be very good. Everyone is dreadfully out of practice.

I have entered for the Science Prize this year. The only other entrants are Higgs and Saxby who have both been in the VI for about 3 years, so I don't stand much of a chance. I have done the Physics part already. It was "Investigate the oscillation of a pendulum in the form of a uniform rod, when the plane of the oscillation is inclined to the vertical".

I have just started the chemistry. We are given a hunk of metal which we have to analyse, and then find the % composition of it.

Isn't the news from Italy marvellous? I expect we will be in Rome soon.

We aren't having a proper Whit half-day. Monday's afternoon lessons are being transferred to Tuesday.

* * *

Sunday 4th June 1944

Thank you very much for your letter. The hot spell was scorching here. I was at the baths a lot. The temperature went up to 72º F, but it has gone down again now. I have learned to dive and pick things off the gratings at the bottom by diving, and apart from bringing up rocks, leaves etc., I brought up a pioneer corps badge and a waterlogged conker. Uufortunately I did not have enough time to get sunburned.

The declamation prize has been won by Higgs one of the VI_3 representatives. (He is also a swimming prefect).

Our first XI played Trent college at cricket yesterday (away). It is the match of the season. The match was a draw. Each side got 111 runs all out. We would have won had it not been for the fact that a drive by Mason hit the shooting stick on which the umpire was sitting and they were only able to run 1 instead of 2. Our captain made 51. He was caught on the boundary.

Lane has now nothing to do with the bugles. He has resigned because he is learning to play the oboe. The weight of the Retreat will fall greatly on my shoulders.

Do you want me to pay for the watch? If so take the cash out of my post office savings account. Please could you send it to me as soon as possible. I feel lost without it.

Did you buy anything with my money when you were in Stratford? I hope it was something nice.

I'm glad to hear that the insurance company is standing the racket with regard to the wireless set.

There were a lot of people over on Whit Sunday. I walked over to Braunston on Saturday. The heat nearly killed me.

I was on duty all last week. (I had to ring the bell at 5 to 8 and all the other ones as well, read the roll-call, take prep and lock up at night). It was a strain ringing the bell at 5 minutes to 8. I usually don't get up till about 3 minutes to.

As you know, I entered for the science prize. The chemistry was all right but the other two have had more time on it, and my results are wrong. I could however have rectified them if I had had more time. As it was I spent nine hours on it last week. Still, it was good practice for me.

PS. I am playing Bach's Aria in a concert at the end of term (also called "Air on the G string"). One boy in my dormitory has got mumps.

It's terrific news about the Normandy landings, but the Germans have got these new flying bombs, which sound very bad. We were in a very good mood and Lane took a photo of all the front of house gang (seniors and prefects).

8. Wharflands — the Front of House gang, June 1944
Front row, L to R: Frisby; Hopewell; Meakin; Jacobs; Dilks; Wilson; Iley; Whitlock. Back Row, L to R: Mockford; Mason; Stanton; Wright

* * *

Sunday 18/6/44

Thank you for your letter. What do you think of the pilotless bomber? I think that it will very soon be stopped by very powerful British transmitters which will turn them round or something like that.

I competed for the Fenwick cup for shooting. Lane got it with a score of 79/80. I only got 42/85 (I came 13th).

I was in a Wharflands team of 4 which shot against an equal

school house team on Thursday. It was a draw with 246 each (I scored 40/85). [lousy!]

It was shot again today. We won by 1 point. We got 135 they got 134. I shot better this time, getting 32/50. So Wharflands has now 2 more cups to add to the steadily growing collection.

I haven't been in the baths again yet, but I might today. It was 62°F yesterday.

We had a miniature heat wave yesterday it was baking in the baths. The temperature went up 1° in an hour. There was quite a wind, but the walls of the baths screened it.

P.S. Speech day invitation enclosed.

* * *

Sunday, 25th June 1944

Thank you for your letters. We had field day on Thursday and it was most tiring. We got transport in American lorries out to Cold Overton, a village about 3½ miles from Oakham. I was leading "1 Group". This consisted of two tommy-gunners, two riflemen and a wireless operator. We were sent out as a hit and run reconnaissance patrol. We set out OK, but after a few hundred yards our operator lost contact with control at Cold Overton. (It wasn't our fault). We advanced out of the wood after waiting 5 minutes static in an unsuccessful attempt to re-establish communication. We then moved through the wood down the right bank of the stream. I had just found a nice position to defend, and was placing my men when we were wiped out by fire from the other side of a hedge on the other side of the stream. We went back with the people who had shot us up, and joined in with the attack. Whitlock's section and mine were left in a defensive position, and the other attacking sections moved off saying that they would send a runner to tell us when to move on. We waited 40 minutes, but no runner came, so we retraced out steps using all the woodcraft etc., we knew and by the time we reached Cold Overton, we found that it had all been over for almost ¾ of an hour. Were we sore? We did a smaller scheme in the afternoon which was not really of note.

I am in the Wharflands section, for the section shield. It is being led by Lane.

On Tuesday I shot on the open range again, and Lane (who is the best shot in the school) and I, shot point for point on each group application etc. We finished up with 64 out of 75. First class (open) is 52. I used a P.14 again. I need the better sights, and found that I could hit the bull by firing at the bottom left hand corner of the target!

I swam yesterday and on Field Day. The temperature has been slowly but surely mounting all the week. It is now 65½° F. I am learning the technique of diving. Proctor says I'm good. I do a good one occasionally, but mostly the back of my legs hit the water with a smack.

Please could Mum bring my boater when she comes over on Speech Day. I shall need it at the baths. I can't think of anything else that might come in handy. I'm afraid I won't be able to meet Mum at 3 p.m., but I can arrive at the Crown at about 5 or 10 past 4. At 8 p.m. I regret to say, I will be taking prep in the hut. I may have to wait till morning before I can see you.

I am sorry Dad can't come over for Speech Day, I think he would have enjoyed it.

The lime trees are not in bloom yet, and I haven't seen the tail end of a strawberry or cherry. I don't think the Retreat will be as good as last year but we will do our best.

Back at home for the holidays now. Dad has come up with a great idea. One of the people he knows through the bank has told him about the Nuffield Apprenticeship scheme. This is the best possible news, as I should get to work on cars. Brilliant!

I had a nice invitation to go to Lincoln for a few days during the hols to stay with Michael Whitlock and his parents at their house in Lincoln. It will be just like old times, as we used to live there and there were lots of parties.

Postcard — Tuesday 15/8/44

I arrived safely at Lincoln after a rather hectic journey at 7 p.m. I caught the 1.15 as the 1.25 was running 25 minutes late at Cheltenham. Arrived Derby at 3.20 left at 3.20. Arrived Nottingham at 4.40 left 5.23, and finally arrived in Lincoln at 7. It all seems rather changed here but I knew my way about. I saw Stella Thirkell from afar last night. The Whitlocks have got a lovely huge house, which is spotlessly clean. Mrs Whitlock is very nice. The food is par excellence. We are going up the cathedral today. Michael has had a cyst removed but is OK.

Lincoln was super, but the rail journey back to Birmingham was a bit of a performance, with a change of trains at Nottingham. Dad has been busy while I've been away and it seems that there's a possibility I could join the Nuffield scheme at the Wolseley factory here in Birmingham They've sent lots of bumf about it and Dad is going to get in touch with GTG to see what he thinks.

Not much holiday left now, as I shall be back at Oakham in a few days.

Year Six

Autumn 1944 — Summer 1945

24th September 1944

Thanks very much indeed for the parcel and your good
wishes. It arrived safely yesterday. The cake is lovely, fruit
and sweets ditto but the biscuits taste rather ancient. The
cake I came away with was lovely; it was cooked quite long
enough.

Thank you very much indeed for the golf clubs and the
season ticket. They will be most welcome (I am just being
formal).

On Tuesday the train arrived on time (approx). I then
ambled up to Wharflands and looked over the 2 motorbikes
and the Bren gun which the J.T.C. has just received. I started
up one of the bikes. The other was in need of repair so on
Thursday night a boy called Wright and myself dragged it
out and repaired it. I had a ride round the Wharflands Quad
on it, and losing control sailed out and nearly rammed a
henhouse.

We have been cleaning corps equipment all the week as a
squad of 20 from our J.T.C. (me included) went to Leicester
yesterday to the de Montfort Hall where the Leicestershire
regiment was presented with the freedom of the city.
General Liddel accepted the scroll from the Mayor. The
whole rigmarole was recorded by the B.B.C. There were
present a guard of honour from the Leicestershires whose
drill was the snappiest I have ever seen, an old soldiers
detachment, members of Leicestershire cadet forces and
Home Guard battalions, 20 Uppingham cadets who were
jolly decent, (I talked to some of them) and ourselves. There

were also 3 bands. We then marched through Leicester for about 3 miles with fixed bayonets (the only cadets who did so; Uppingham cadets hadn't even got any rifles) and Captain Cox was on the saluting base. He said we were smarter than any of the other cadets, and than most of the Home Guards. Just past the saluting base was a B.B.C. chap howling into a mike on top of a recording van. He was urging the crowd to cheer by waving a piece of paper frantically at them. Although I says it as who shouldn't we were very smart. We had tea afterwards at a W.V.S. canteen. We went to Leicester and came back in an army lorry.

Today the Drums marched the scouts of Rutland (also the guides and cubs) round the town on their way to a memorial service for Lord Somers the Chief Scout. It was bitterly cold. (I am writing this letter in a battledress, two sweaters and an overcoat).

By the way, I am now a school prefect, and I will read the lesson in the chapel for the first time at the evening service next Sunday and for the following week.

I have got the socks and things from F & H's.

G.T.G. is making enquiries about engineering drawing at Uppingham, Melton, Stamford and Oakham. As yet no replies have been received.

Please thank Mrs Green very much indeed for me for sending the sweets. they are most welcome to a poor, starving, schoolboy.

I am now in charge of Lower 10 dormitory and <u>so far</u> they have been quite well behaved.

I am still sharing a study with Lane who is now a school prefect and head of Wharflands.

We weep bitterly on each others shoulders when H.Sc.Cert is mentioned.

I am settling down to work with a will, quote "I did Saturday's prep on Thursday".

GTG has been very helpful with the whole engineering idea. It's really very decent of him as he's really a dyed in the wool scripture and classics man.. He's got me into an engineering drawing class at Melton Mowbray Technical College. It will happen every Friday evening, so I'll have to get there and back on the train and miss prep. Is that wonderful news or what?

Tuesday 3/10/44

Thank you for the parcel. I am afraid this letter will be very brief as I am writing it before chapel.

I start night classes at Melton on Friday, please could you see if you could get me some drawing instruments for this? There aren't any decent ones in Oakham.

On Sunday night I read the lesson in chapel. I felt a bit shaky as I went up, but when I was reading it was all right. I had practiced it well, (although I says it as who shouldn't). I was complimented by all and sundry, and Proctor said it was one of the best if not the best read lesson he had heard in the chapel.

My dear dormitory remembered that I had had a birthday last night, and so I was bumped 16 times with great ceremony. It's a cruel 'ard life! Everyone in the dormitory concerned is bumped on his birthday.

The smashed corps motor bike has just been repaired. It is better than the other one was.

We picked potatoes last Monday morning, instead of school, and ditto in the afternoon after school.

On Wednesday I played my first game of rugger this term. It was quite good, but rather tiring. I played again on Thursday. I enjoyed that game more than the other.

On Friday we did Corps. Nothing spectacular. On Saturday I watched an Old Boys match. They beat us about 20 – 0. They were almost all old Colours.

So far I have raked in about 40/-. Please put the cash you have got in the P.O. saving bank.

* * *

Sunday 8/10/44

Thank you for your letter and the parcel. The instruments will be fine. I have managed to get a ruler.

I read the lesson all this week, and I have got quite used to it now. I had a very nice set of lessons as a matter of fact.

On Tuesday I was one of a shooting 8 which shot against the A.T.C. we used rifles and Lewis guns. We won by 192 points to 147.

I shot my empire test on Wednesday. I got 56 out of 70. (1st class)

The Drums have been practicing again, and I am wondering whether or not to leave, as my playing is not all it used to be. I will see if I can improve it by practice.

On Friday I went to Melton on the 6.15 train. I was able to find the college all right, and after an interview with the principal went into the engineering drawing class. I had to make a working sketch of a simple bearing, and then make a full size front elevation, plan, end elevation and section of it from the drawing. It was quite easy. The other lads there were jolly decent. I enjoyed the class immensely. Afterwards I indulged in an orgy of fish and chips, and then caught the 9.55 train back.

Today we shot against the A.T.C. with Lewis guns. It was pouring with rain. There were 10 in each team, and we had 20 shots each. We beat then by 60 to 28. I got 6 out of 20. (Highest score 10)

The study decorating is going according to plan. We have started a craze. Have you managed to get my wallpaper yet?

* * *

15th October 1944

Thank you for your letters. I got my identity card etc. OK. If Graham Donovan does produce a book on engineering drawing, thank him very much from me and send it on. It will probably come in handy.

On Friday night I went to Melton again and carried on with the drawing I had started the previous time. It is nearly finished now. I had some more fish and chips afterwards, and got back at 10.30. I had a piece of tart and 2 rock buns when I got in. They know at Melton that I am taking Higher Cert in engineering drawing. I think I will be all right.

I asked Mrs Burton yesterday about staying the weekend, but she has a permanent lodger in the room Mum slept in, and so she can't manage it. I will make enquiries at The Roebuck. Is Dad coming over on the 17th of November?

Actually, the trip to Melton Mowbray technical college is turning out to be more educational than I expected. On the late train back to Oakham afterwards there are quite a few American soldiers and their girlfriends. They spend all their time drinking and snogging!

Tuesday 17/10/44

Sorry I couldn't finish the letter on Sunday but I had some urgent prep to do.

I went to the "Roebuck" today, and they can give Mum bed and breakfast on Saturday and Sunday 29th and 30th of October (or any weekend I think). Let me know if you can't come then as I have booked for you.

On Thursday we had Field Day. I was in command of a

section in defence in a trackless wood (it measured about 1¼ mile by ¾ mile). We succeeded in surrounding 2 attacking sections as they advanced, and from good natural cover succeeded in wiping them up. I was most pleased (I also had a man or two by way of reinforcements)

On Thursday night we went to a lecture on the Tennessee Valley Authority with lantern slides. It was given by an American with a rich resonant voice called Mr Grant.

We were going to do tactics in Corps today, but it rained so we did fire orders indoors instead.

On Sunday Night Lane and I went to Mr Cox's home for supper. We had tomato soup, meat pie (lovely!) with swedes, carrots and potatoes, and then lemon curd tart and jam tart, followed by Ryvita, cheese, celery and coffee. It was jolly good.

I haven't started to learn on the motor bikes yet, as the insurance policies for us haven't come through yet. (We'll probably need them!)

P.S. If you can find a book or two of mine which I have read, and not of particular interest to me (in your opinion) please send it/them on, and I will put it/them in the house library, as we are trying to increase the size by this means, and everyone is contributing.

* * *

Sunday Oct. 22nd 1944

Thank you for your letter. Nothing spectacular has happened this week.

I am pleased to hear that Mum can come over on the 29th.

On Thursday I was made captain of 2nd Lot (and of the 3rd XV)

On Friday there was Corps. We did fire orders.

On Friday night I went to Melton as usual, and finished my drawing of a simple bearing. I will start drawing a complicated casting next week. I do one or two small very rough drawings when (if) I have time.

On Saturday the 3rd XV played Kingswood 4th XV. They were all much bigger than we were but we did very well considering. They beat us 15 – 6. They were rather nice blokes.

This afternoon we shot against the Home Guard. We beat them quite nicely, but I have forgotten the exact scores. The H.G. provided a wizard tea. I scored 62/100.

P.S. I envy your dinner at the Midland Hotel.

Mum came over for the weekend and it was great to see her. We walked about a bit and they looked after her well at The Roebuck. I'm afraid I got a bit slack with letter writing after her visit, but hope to avoid a ticking-off.

Tuesday 28th Nov. '44

Thank you for the letter and the copy of the "Messiah". I am sorry I did not write to you on Sunday, but I was working all afternoon at the Magazine.

Last Tuesday the Corps motor-bikes were taken out on the field as the insurance had come, and I managed to start one which they thought was a dud one, and rode it round the field. (As I wasn't yet an N.C.O. this was illegal, but Mr Cox didn't mind). I had a sergeant in the Corps on the pillion, and overtook the boy who was riding the other bike. It was wizard.

On Tuesday night I was sick, so I went to bed early. I was sick twice more in the night, and so I stayed out of school till Friday.

Today we took Cert 'A' part 2. We did Drill, Map-Reading

and Weapon Training this morning, and Battle Drill and Tactics this afternoon. Everyone got through with 3 exceptions in School House. Lane tells me that I got top marks, but this is not yet official. The results will not be up till tomorrow morning (Lane is C.S.M.). The exam wasn't too bad at all, the examiners were jolly decent. They told us that the actual certificate will come through later.

* * *

Monday 4th Dec, 1944

Thank for your letter, the Y.H.A. Map, membership card, The Rucksack and so on.

I am sorry I didn't write on Sunday, but I was in the San, and I didn't come out till today.

On Wednesday night I felt groggy after a bath, and got some Sal Volatile from Matron (Ugh!) But at Thursday lessons I didn't feel so good, and retired to Matron before lunch. I had quite a high temperature on Thursday night, and went into the San on Friday morning. I came out this morning, after walking to Brooke village and back. I am quite OK now.

On Sunday the Home Guard had a Standing Down parade through the town at which the Drums and the Rutland Constabulary band assisted. (I have left the drums by the way).

I am very busy with the Magazine now, as I was in the San on the weekend.

The boy who went home on his bike had apparently run away; he came back for two days and then went again. I don't know why. He has gone to see a Psychologist.

Next term's Wharflands play is going to be "The Housemaster".

* * *

Sunday 10th Dec. 1944

Thank you for the letter. I am glad Dad liked the golf balls. Thanks for Mum's offer of a driver. I would like one very much. The yeast is doing my spots good, thanks.

I'm itching for a game of golf with Dad at Moseley. I'll show him!

Please could Mum bring my skates to the station when she meets me on the 19th.

Nothing really spectacular has happened this week.

On Friday, however, we went to see "This Happy Breed" at the "County" instead of afternoon school. I had seen it before with you but I enjoyed seeing it again. The whole school went and we were in the balcony which we completely filled. The Central School and other elementary schools in the district went downstairs.

In Corps the same day, we had a lecture on "The Indian Army" by Colonel Baxter. We were also shown a film about the training of the Indian (native) soldier.

On Friday night I went to Melton as usual. I am now drawing a cylinder and gland for a steam engine.

It has been a rush all week with the magazine because I was in the San, but I think it will all come right in the end.

It snowed hard this afternoon about 1½" of snow fell. It is raining now and the snow is melting.

Back to Birmingham for Christmas and a much better atmosphere at home. Everyone is more cheerful, now that we're pushing the Germans back in Europe.

Lots more ice skating too, and several visits to the Edwards'.

Monday 22 Jan. '45

Thanks for the letter card. I had quite a reasonable journey, the train arrived at Oakham at about 3 o'clock. I went to Woodcocks for tea with Dudley, and afterwards we went to the "Royal" to see "Song of the open Road". It was a musical film and it was pretty awful but it was a good way to spend the time.

My trunk was a bit mashed up on the way here, but I think I'll be able to patch it up.

Lane has brought some wallpaper back, we have wallpapered the study and it looks quite nice now. We were finishing it on Sunday night, and that's why I didn't write then. We started operations on Thursday, and got the fags to clean the carpets.

As I am keeping a diary, and referring to it for this letter, I will continue this letter in diary form.

Friday

There was a dreadful gale last night (100 m.p.h. according to the wireless), and it took me ages to get to sleep.

Went to the first Corps parade of the term. I learned that I was acting corporal (2 stripes on each arm) the only one of last term's candidates to hold such a high rank (ta-ra-ta-ra). I am in command of the signals section.

I went to Melton with Mockford (he is starting going to the 'Tec' too). We had our usual fish and chips afterwards.

Saturday

Snow fell last night. We rehearsed "Housemaster" all the afternoon (I read it in the train coming back here). A lot more snow fell in the afternoon. Two other boys and myself have decided to see if there is any skating tomorrow.

Sunday

Froze last night. Jacobs, Sutton and I went skating on Burley swamps in the afternoon. It was very rough and rather thin ice but we quite enjoyed it. I lent my skates to Jacobs.

<u>Monday</u>

More snow fell last night, and it froze. Lane and I went sledging this afternoon on Mr Cox's sledge, we had a jolly good time, but were completely wrecked as it was very bumpy and very steep, and we fell off a good bit. We were late for tea but nobody seemed to mind. I am on duty this week.

The orange cake is lovely; I didn't cut it until today.

I have got some more of that lotion made up.

Now I'm in charge of the signals section I can get the Corps radios whenever I want to. So, at the end of the week, I 'borrowed' a couple of No. 18 sets which were temporarily installed in the common room at the top of the Hut, where I hooked them up to a record player. Just outside were the aerials for all the battery radio sets in the studies at the back of the house, so I hooked the No. 18s onto those too. We managed to get such a powerful signal that the boys in School House could hear us on <u>Medium Wave.</u>

In no time at all we had set up a radio station — a sort of 'twin' to the American Forces Network. We had a signature tune, Benny Goodman's 'Six Flats Unfurnished' and I played requests, mostly numbers by Harry James, Tommy Dorsey, Woody Herman, Glen Miller and Lionel Hampton. After two days, though, we decided to close down and put the sets back before we were discovered — there would have been the most terrible row — but it was fun while it lasted.

Sunday 28th Jan. '45

Thank you for your letter. My share in the Wallpaper cost 6/-. It is mostly a warm shade of brown with a red and green pattern. It is admired by all.

Neither Snipper nor Bowman have returned this term.

My spots are about as when I went back, if anything slightly better. the lotion is good stuff.

We got three oranges each yesterday. I ate them all after tea.

Thanks for the cutting. I showed it to Proctor.

I am still writing my diary, so I will continue the letter in diary form.

<u>Tuesday</u>

It froze last night and snowed all the morning and early afternoon. I went sledging on Cold Overton hill with Proctor and Lane. We borrowed Mr Cox's sledge. We had a lovely time and Mrs Cox gave us some lovely cake. Had a bath in cold water. We had a Corps parade in the afternoon and we took the wireless out.

<u>Wednesday</u>

Froze again last night, so we went skating on Burley Swamps in the afternoon, but we didn't have time to clear much snow, although the ice underneath was like glass. I went for a music lesson in the evening.

<u>Thursday</u>

It froze again last night, so I went skating again. Mr Moore was there, he's not a bad skater, and we had a good time. Jim Adcock (he stokes the boiler) is ill, so the pipes are cold.

<u>Friday</u>

Another freeze last night. We took the wirelesses out in Corps and I broadcast some records from the top of the hut. Went to Melton, where I had an exam, and did (for me) rather well, I think. The train was an hour late on the way back.

<u>Saturday</u>

The water pipes froze last night. I went skating on the Burley Fishponds with Proctor, Mr and Mrs Cox and many others. We got labour squads clearing snow, and I danced the Waltz and Twostep with Mrs Cox, also giving advice in three dances to Mr Cox. Had a smashing time, the ice was marvellous.

Sunday

We went skating on Burley Fishponds again, and I danced with Mrs Cox. The Head Man was there as well, he attempts to figure skate like Mr Moore. It wasn't quite as good as yesterday but I quite enjoyed it. I read the lesson in chapel. Proctor said it was first class. I turned on full volume for a denunciatory bit at the end. (Ta-ra; ta-ra!)

Monday

Froze again last night. I went to the Burley Fishponds, but there wasn't time to do any skating. We had a practice for the "Messiah" during prep. It nearly killed me, as the tenor part is awfully high.

Today

Six inches of snow fell last night but it has nearly all thawed now. We took out the 18's in Corps today, and afterwards we listened to British and American aircraft over Frankfurt, and coming back to land, also some glider tugs, troops and transport (civil?) aircraft. It was very interesting. I had to read the lesson at short notice this morning, because the boy who should have read it was away. We are painting the study and are in a state of chaos.

P.S. Sorry I didn't finish on Sunday night, but we had a "Housemaster" rehearsal, and I hadn't time yesterday. I apologise for the scrawl, but I should be in bed now, so I'm in a hurry.

* * *

Tuesday 6/2/45

Thanks for your letters. As you have probably heard by now I am in the San. I will tell you more later. Thank you very much for the 10/- note – it is helping to cover the expenses of painting and decorating. I expect Lane has just about finished it now. The study has been admired by all.

I will continue as usual in diary form.

<u>Wednesday</u>

Thawed during the night. It is very slippery. We had a lecture this morning in the old School by a Major. He was talking about the Sicily landings. After tea I got in touch with Mr Cox by morse on a number 18 set. It is the first time they have been used for morse.

<u>Thursday</u>

Thawed some more last night. There is hardly any snow left now. I went on a run to the second bridge on the Burley road. I quite enjoyed it. We had a rehearsal of the Housemaster Act 1 Scene 1. I know quite a lot of it now.

<u>Friday</u>

Hardly a trace of snow left now. Did No. 18 procedure in J.T.C. Mr Cox and I are trying to mend a connector cord for the sets. I have got rather a chill and a hacking cough but I went to Melton, and found that I came 3rd in the exam with 80%. When I got back, my chill was worse so I had a couple of aspirins before going to bed.

<u>Saturday</u>

I was feeling a bit groggy so I stayed in bed and I was packed off to the San. I had a temperature of 100.2º F. I read "Prince of the Captivity" by John Buchan. Got a letter from Mum. Temperature in the evening 101.2ºF.

<u>Sunday</u>

Temp. 99.5ºF. corn Flakes, Bread, butter and Marmite for breakfast. I am reading "Happy-go-Lucky" by Ian Hay. Scrambled eggs and pudding for lunch. Finished book. Started "Quinney's Adventures". Temp. 99.2ºF.

<u>Monday</u>

Normal Temperature (98.4ºF). Had sore throat first thing,

which soon vanished. Finished reading "Quinney's Adventures". Started "Ghosts and Marvels" (Short Stories). Started to itch like anything towards evening, otherwise quite OK. Temperature 99ºF

Tuesday

Temp. Normal. Finished "Ghosts and Marvels". Read "The Three Coffins". Got a letter from Dad. I was itching again, so I was swilled down with Calamine Lotion. I appear to have Urticaria or something. It's driving me crazy. Temp. Normal.

Wednesday

Temp. Normal. Read a book called "Among Chinese Pirates", one of these "boy hero" books. It was awful. I am constantly learning my part, and I am also writing a funny (?) story. I'll let you see it when its finished.

I'm afraid I won't be able to get the trouser measurements till I'm released. 2 or 3 days.

I hope Mum is better now.

P.S. Please excuse writing. I'm in bed.

* * *

Tuesday 13th Feb. '45

Thanks for your letter. I am quite hale and hearty and restored to as near normal as I ever am. I come out of the San on Friday.

I got the measurements from F & H on Friday. Here they are:-

44" — Side Seam

30½" — Leg Finished

30" — Waist

39" — Seat

22" — Knee

20" — Bottom

I will continue the letter, as per usual, in diary form.

Thursday

Temp. Normal. I got up today and went down to the Day-Room (at the San) I read "Ivanhoe". I will probably go out tomorrow. Temp. Normal

Friday

Got up and went shopping for the San matron and went back to Wharflands for lunch. We have got some new wireless sets which arrived during corps. We have 2 of them. They are massive things, and have a range of about 100 miles. They are number 11 sets. I wasn't allowed to go to Melton because I had just come out of the San.

Saturday

I had a leave off games, so I went for a long walk in the afternoon and took a couple of panoramas of Oakham from the surrounding mountains'. Mr Cox gave me a 6 – 20 film because it wouldn't fit his camera. Bung Ho! We have to use a code with these new sets because they are so powerful. We have also been given a call-sign.

Sunday

Shot in the miniature range this afternoon for practice for the "Country Life" competition.

It snowed this afternoon. But nearly all the snow had gone by evening. I spoke to Mr Cox at his house from Wharflands using one of the 11's. They are a bit tricky to handle, but I'm getting the hang of them. I read the lesson in chapel. It was full of unpronounceable names, but I managed all right.

Monday

Its raining like anything, so there will be no hockey this afternoon. We went for a run to Ashwell crossroads, however. I wrote a story while I was in the San. I'm considering sending it up.

Tuesday

No P.T. because it was raining hard. I read my story to Proctor. He approves of it and appears to like it. We have got the special records of sound effects for the "Housemaster" they are rather peculiar, being made of glass. In corps this afternoon we had a lecture on the new code, and on the 11 sets. After corps I went for a run with Lane. We had a rehearsal for the "Housemaster" after tea. I pretty well know my part now.

I am sorry I didn't write on Sunday, but I was rather busy as you have seen.

My rash and itching have completely disappeared but I still have a bit of a cold. They think the cause of the rash was Soda Sal, a vile sort of medicine they gave me to get my temperature down. Its proper name is Sodium Salicylate.

I will see about private lessons next term, but I think the evening classes still carry on.

There seems to be a black market in oranges here. I will see if I can get some for you.

I will be looking forward to seeing Mum on the 3rd of March.

My shoes are quite watertight thanks.

I enclose the measurements as written by the tailor at F & H. in case there is any question about any of the measurements.

I am on duty for reading the lesson this week.

* * *

Sunday 18th Feb. 1945

Thanks for your letter. You seem to have had a good time at that dance. Birmingham seems to have gone festive all of a sudden.

I am glad to hear that Mum is OK now. I am keeping well

except for a cough.

What is Paula training for? I didn't know she was at a business college.

I'm afraid that when I turned up at the shop all the oranges had been sold.

Thanks for your promise of tuck. It will be very welcome.

There hasn't been any spectacular happening this week, but I will continue as per usual.

Wednesday

Went to the baths this afternoon for labour. I helped to get the cover plates off the tank full of sand which does the filtering. There are over 20,000 holes in the bottom of this tank and we will have to take the sand out and then get in and prick each one with some pointed implement. It will take weeks. I went for a music lesson in the evening.

Thursday

I played my first game of hockey (this term) this afternoon. I enjoyed it very much, but split my stick down the middle. Went to choir practice afterwards, and we practiced some new hymns. Lane is in bed today.

Friday

I mended my hockey stick with insulation tape. In corps today we did no.11 procedure. I went to Melton with Mockford. I learned there that the 'Tec' might open in the summer, or it might close as far as drawing was concerned, depending on the demand. They will let me know. I have paid the entrance fee for an exam which takes place on April 14th from 2 till 6 at Melton. It is in Drawing, and if I get through it will give me a year's start at the 'Tec' which I will be going to while I am at Wolseley. Inter BSc saves me two years, but this will certainly help me along. I hope this is OK with you. Mockford has offered to put me up for the night after the exam. He lives at Leicester and will be taking it too.

Saturday

Played hockey again this afternoon. (did I tell you I was captain of Second lot?) As there weren't many people there, we amalgamated with 3rd lot and picked up sides. It was a jolly good game and resulted in a draw.

I don't think there's much more news except that I know my part now. I think we will start riding the motor bikes soon. I'll send you a carbon copy of the story when I type it out. It is a school story and I'm thinking of sending it to the "Boy's Own Paper".

Proctor sends his kind regards.

* * *

Sunday 25th Feb. '45

Thanks very much indeed for the parcel and the letter. I really did enjoy that parcel especially the cake. It didn't take long to polish it off.

Please could you bring my suit over, and Dad's Dinner Jacket and Waistcoat. Proctor can lend me some trousers. Could you also bring a white cricket shirt and a black bow tie if possible.

I'll see about the clothing coupons.

There are stacks of crocuses (croci?) out here. They look very nice.

We are having Field Day on Tuesday, and we are going to a place where there are all sorts of mineral railways and quarries.

I have typed out my story, and Proctor has corrected it, but I don't see myself getting time to type it out I'm afraid at least not for a few weeks. I will send you a carbon copy when I finish it.

<u>Tuesday</u>

Sorry I didn't get time to finish on Sunday, but we had a

rehearsal in the afternoon. I will now proceed as usual.

Monday

We played hockey today. It wasn't a bad game.

Tuesday

The parcel arrived. I have already expressed my thanks etc. etc. In Corps I did some revolver shooting at the miniature range, and had a ride on one of the motor bikes. I managed all right, and didn't fall off or anything. I found an old large scale map of Oakham and environs, which someone had drawn. It is very old and faded, so I am rejuvenating it.

Wednesday

Laboured at the baths today. We have now emptied the sand out of the filter tank, and the hole-pricking will begin soon. Went for a music lesson as usual.

Thursday

Had a wizard game of hockey this afternoon. The score was 4 – 4. I really enjoyed it, as I was able to be some really good "golf shots". Went to Choir practice and sang "Messiah" and new hymns. I have seen people about with grapefruits which they have bought in town.

Friday

In corps tested batteries and sets for field day. Went to Melton as usual. I tried to get a grapefruit before corps, but they were sold out.

Saturday

Went to Braunston for tea with David (Lane). We had eggs and cake galore, and a mountain of bread and butter. We had a huge basin of sugar and a lovely big pot of tea. It cost us 1/3 each. There was a hockey match against the Paratroops (They have taken over from the Americans at Ashwell camp, North of Oakham). We lost 4 – 2.

Sunday

I read one of the lessons in Morning Chapel. We had a rehearsal of the entire play in the afternoon. It lasted 3½ hours. We had ½ a grapefruit each for breakfast! They were lovely. Proctor turned on his charm and managed to get some. I can't though.

<u>Monday</u>

Played hockey this afternoon. It was quite a good game. During prep we had a Messiah practice with the Choral Society in the Drawing School. I managed to get higher than usual. (The tenor part is absolutely wrecking).

<u>Tuesday</u>

Field Day today. we started off after chapel, and I was attached to 8 platoon, and had a wireless set (No.18) and a cadet to help me with it, plus an acting L/Cpl. with a smaller set, who was to go on reconnaissance patrols. We took up our position round a huge impenetrable wood, but we had too few men, and were defeated.

In the afternoon we attacked another wood. I was with a small wireless set in a "suicide squad" which was to locate the enemy. We got to within 10 yards of their positions before they saw us, and then we were in a perfect defensive position on a railway line, between some loaded iron ore trucks and a stack of coal. The attack was a success.

I enclose my certificate 'A' and another one, certificate 'T' for technical work. Also I'm sending a carbon copy of the <u>uncorrected</u> version of my story, and the map of Oakham which I told you about.

I am looking forward to seeing Mum on Saturday.

* * *

Sunday 11th March 1945

Thanks for the letter card. I enjoyed the weekend very much indeed.

Treen is out of the San now. He appears to be quite all right.

We have had exams this week, and as far as I know, I haven't done too badly.

I can't think of any more blather at the moment so I'll continue as usual with the weekly communiqué from G.H.Q. Rutland.

<u>Monday</u>

We had our Statics exam this morning. It was a pretty stiff paper. I talked to Mr Cox and Proctor about stage props after afternoon school. Then I went on a run to a pill-box on the Ashwell Road. We had a rehearsal after tea.

<u>Tuesday</u>

I came 2nd in the Statics exam with 45% (pass). It was an old Higher Cert paper. In Corps I instructed people in the use of the 'Don 5' field telephone. We had an Algebra and Trigonometry exam this morning. It was rather easier than the other one. I started to type out the fair copy of my story after Corps.

<u>Wednesday</u>

I came 2nd in the Alg. and Trig. Exam with 67%. We had English and German exams today. After school I did labour, rolling the cricket pitches. We had another play rehearsal after tea.

<u>Thursday</u>

I got 61% in German – I was second. the boy who was first got 62%. I came second in English, I haven't seen the marks, but I hear that I got somewhere in the seventies.

We had a Chemistry test (not exam) in the morning. After lunch I went for a run to the Burley Swamps, across to the Burley Road and back. after that I went to choir practice.

<u>Friday</u>

Had a Co-Ordinate Geometry exam this morning. It was dreadfully stiff. I posted my story to Lilliput this morning. We did 'Don 5's' and Exchange in Corps. I went to Melton as usual. They were sold out of fish, so we had peas and double chips.

<u>Saturday</u>

This afternoon I rode on the newer of the two Motor Bikes. I changed up and went quite fast on it. I went to Braunston with Lane on borrowed bikes and had the usual tea with eggs.

<u>Sunday</u>

After lunch, I did some practice shooting for the "Country Life" competition. I am writing this letter in the middle of a rehearsal, which is lasting from 2.30 till 5.30.

Has anything been done about the artesian well in the Garden?

How many strokes did Dad take in his round of golf?

I can't think of any more news at the moment, and I'm due on the stage in a moment, so I will close now.

P.S. I enclose corrected first edition, and final edition of my story.

My last Easter holiday while I'm still at school, so did the same sort of things — skating and visiting the Edwards'. Paula and Mariane are getting quite grown up now (and I suppose I am too). I went to a church youth club in Moseley a couple of times, where there were some smashing girls. There was table tennis and dancing and everyone was very friendly.

Dad took me for an interview at the Wolseley factory on the east side of Birmingham. We met the Apprentice Supervisor, Mr Coshall, and also the boss of the whole scheme throughout the Nuffield Organisation, Mr. Moyle. They said that there would be a place for me if I did well enough in my exams, so fingers crossed. This will be my last term — back to Oakham soon.......

Sunday 6th May 1945

We arrived safely at Oakham at about 8 o'clock after quite a

good journey straight through. The ice-cream was lovely and we suffered no ill effects.

We are still not sure whether we will be able to come home on V.E. DAY. If we are I think it would be a kindly and compassionate act to bring Lane with me. Is this OK with you?

Please could you ask Mr Newman if he would send the wireless set he is getting for Proctor here. It should be a 'Pilot' set (made in U.S.A.). a cheque will be forthcoming.

We are now well established and ready to get down to work. Yesterday we had the usual beginning of term service, and a little time with form masters. We filled bottles in the Labs.

All Saturday afternoon it poured with rain, but in spite of that I strolled round the town. I went to Furley and Hassans, but they have no black coats that will fit me. I got a pair of braces (price 2/4).

In the right hand pocket of my black overcoat there is a small pocket which <u>may</u> contain a close-up lens for my camera. If you can find it there please could you send it to me. (Don't bother to look anywhere else).

P.S. Went to usual Sunday service this morning.

It was absolutely wizard to have a holiday to celebrate V.E. Day. The Head Man gave us all two days off, so that we could go home. Unfortunately for some boys this wasn't possible — like David Lane, so he came home with me. There was a simply amazing party at the Edwards' with lots of music and dancing. We both had a great time, but the journey home was a bit difficult.

Sunday May 13th '45

You will probably be wondering if we got back OK. Well, I will tell you, starting at the beginning.

We arrived at Derby at 6.15 thereby missing our connection to Leicester which left at 6.12. We then went in a body and interviewed the Stationmaster and found that we could get a train to Leicester, Market Harboro and Kettering, and then one from Kettering to Oakham. We got a train from Derby at 7.46 which took is to Kettering. (We had phoned Proctor by the way). We then got the 10.51 from Kettering (the church there was floodlit with red and white lights) and we arrived in Oakham more dead than alive at 11.23. (The train from Kettering was the night train from London to Edinburgh). Proctor gave us some Ovaltine and we staggered into bed. The trains were crammed all the way.

I realised on Thursday that I hadn't got my hairbrush. Thanks very much for sending it. On Thursday I started on the Chemistry part of the Science Prize which I have now completed and written up. We had to determine the percentage of silver in a sixpence. I did this by two different methods and got 46.14% and 47.15% both of which are of the right order. I have not yet written up the Physics.

On Friday I was enlisted as a cymbal player in the Drums in Corps and then we selected people for the House Platoon Shield. I am commanding the Wharflands platoon. (I only have to take them for drill). I have now been made a full corporal.

On Saturday I did chemistry all morning except for a lecture in the Old School by an Old Oakhamian about the Burma Campaign. I finished the chemistry in the afternoon.

Today I played as leading Bugler for a victory parade round the town before going to chapel. We then marched back through the town. We did quite well. I am really out of the Drums, but I turned up to help them out.

Thanks for the information about the wireless. I have passed it on to Proctor.

I have never heard such a good sermon as the Head Man's

this morning, and I have never heard a hymn sung as well as the best one this morning.

We don't have blackout any more, of course, so everything looks very different at night. It's just wonderful to know that things will get back to normal one day. I've heard that Uncle Walter has been posted to Vienna to work on the Allied Control Commission, which sounds very interesting.

Mr. Cox suggested I should put in for a State Scholarship 'just in case', and gave me a form, but it needs to be sent back quickly.

Tuesday 15th May '45

Please could you complete the enclosed form and send it back as soon as possible. I thought I might as well enter because it costs nothing and I needn't accept it.
Please could you tell me Uncle Walter's address in Vienna? I think I might write to him.
I have nearly completed the Physics part of the Science Prize.

* * *

Sunday 20th May '45

Thank you very much indeed for your letters, the State Scholarship form, and the 10/- note, which was just in time to save me from the Bankruptcy Courts.
On Monday I helped Major Hughes to run off some of the heats for the Junior Sports.
On Tuesday I did exactly the same as Monday (exciting isn't it?)
On Wednesday we had a Corps parade and I drilled the Wharflands platoon. My voice is only just beginning to

recover.

On Thursday afternoon I waffled about doing nothing because there wasn't anything to do, and went to choir practice, where I was in no fit state to sing, owing to a sore throat caused by Wednesday's Corps parade.

On Friday it poured all the afternoon but David and I went into Oakham and swanned about for a bit. I made a vain attempt to get my hair cut, the shop being crammed.

Yesterday, Major Hughes, Lane and I looked after the Junior Sports and afterwards we were invited to tea at the Junior House with Mr and Mrs Milliken.

The result of the Science Prize, though not yet officially announced, is I am afraid, adverse. The other bloke beat me by a few marks, according to reports from reliable diplomatic sources.

I am however one of three selected from the sixth form for the Declamation Prize. The other two are Lane and Ridgway.

The parcel was a most welcome surprise. I find strangely enough, that since its arrival I have become very popular! The cake and raisins are especially delicious.

We are not even having a half day at Whit Monday. Isn't it a shame.

Pity about the ice-box. I don't know what we'll do without it. Will have to drink all that milk we get instead of letting it go bad!

I have booked a room at the Crown for the 16th June weekend.

I have got an air letter form, and will write to Uncle Walter sometime.

I will drop a line to Uncle Tom and Auntie Kitty as well.

Please could you see if you can get a diagonal scale in Birmingham, I can't get one here.

I had a phone call with Mum about the diagonal scale to explain exactly what it is. I also asked her if there was any chance at all that I could be allowed to buy a most wonderful three-wheeler which they are selling at the 'Plough' at Braunston. She didn't sound very keen, but said she would ask Dad about it.

Sunday 26th May '45

Thanks very much for the diagonal scale and the letter.

I quite agree with Dad that the 3 wheeler might be a distraction. I suggest however that I might be allowed to buy it if I pass Inter BSc or get exemption from it by means of Inter and Higher Cert. (If I get every subject in Inter, for example, with the exception of chemistry and then obtain a Higher Certificate with a Chemistry pass as a main subject, I am awarded Inter BSc). This would be of invaluable assistance in keeping my nose to the grindstone.

Here are the details, in case Mum forgot any:

B.S.A. three wheeler (2 front, 1 back); front wheel drive; twin cylinder; 4 new tyres; new battery; excellent condition (I have been in, on and around it). Does 45 miles to the gallon. Price £35 (taxed).

You may be interested to hear that for the past week I have done two hours work after lights out every night.

I suppose you haven't had the results of the Melton Exam yet have you?

I think I told Mum on the phone that we didn't get a half holiday on Monday. Poor show wasn't it? I went down to the baths for a bit, and then borrowed Proctor's bike to go to Braunston, where I saw the 3 wheeler but I could get no tea, as they were cleaned out of food.

On Tuesday afternoon I did a lot of painting at the baths and rang up Mum in the evening.

On Wednesday I had just changed for Corps, when as the

result of a friendly brawl during which I dropped my forage cap, I was pushed through a door just as I was about to try to pick my cap up. I went down a step onto a gravel path, and finished up with a severe cut just in my hair above my brow, my brow and nose severely scraped, more scrapes on my left hand and right knee and a bump about the size of a pigeons egg on my brow. I was at once carted off to the San, bleeding like a pig, and after being swathed in bandages and given an anti tetanus injection, I was bundled into bed and kept there overnight. I was back at Wharflands for breakfast.

On Thursday afternoon I went to the baths and did some more painting. we are repainting the diving boards, and it's some job I can tell you.

On Friday it was showery and David went to spy out the land for the Field Day which is on Tuesday. I went to the Plough at Braunston, and David joined me. We had bacon and eggs for tea. (1/- a head) (They hadn't any cakes)

On Friday, instead of afternoon school, we went to see 'Wilson' at the County Cinema. It was very good.

Yesterday afternoon I did some more painting at the Baths. Today nothing spectacular has happened. I will be second in command of the platoon on Field Day, which takes place beyond Brooke village.

* * *

Sunday 3rd June '45

Thank you very much indeed for the lovely parcel. The cakes and things are lovely, and I am thinking of throwing a party for the other prefects with the remnants.

My head is much better now thanks, and bandages etc., were removed last Monday. The only thing is, I had a small patch of hair clipped at the front and, although it is not noticeable, it may take some time to grow.

Sorry if my letter sounded blackmailful but it wasn't meant to be. I was merely following up two remarks which Dad made in his letter. Quote "In other circumstances the proposition might be attractive" and "The vision of a car to dismantle and future scorching along the King's Highway would distract you from your work"; or words to that effect. I was merely combining the two to attempt to provide a solution acceptable to all parties! (I think I should be in the Diplomatic Service, don't you?) Let me repeat once again that no blackmail was implied or intended, and that I deeply regret any misapprehension or misunderstandings caused. I will not refer to the matter again unless invited to do so.

Last Monday I went to the baths and did some painting. Bathing was going to start today, but the weather was foul.

On Tuesday we had a Field Day. David was in charge of the attack which consisted of 3 platoons. I was second in command of one of them. We were attacking 2 platoons in an almost impregnable position. They were holding a road on a ridge, which commanded a terrific view. There were huts along it for use as pillboxes, an actual pillbox, and a disused searchlight emplacement.

We attacked the searchlight with two platoons, but we were thinned out by long range Bren fire, from positions on the ridge. We were also harassed by snipers and machine gun parties in bushes, who opened fire at close range. I ruined one of those sections in that position with two thunderflashes. Then we broke cover, and I raced up the road while the rest lingered behind (I thought they were right on my tail), I was running in the middle of the road for about 150 yards, and I was ten yards from the searchlight emplacement before a shot was fired at me. I threw my thunderflashes at a range of about 3 yards, and nearly blew a bren gunner's trousers off, the thunderflash landing in the middle of the emplacement. (It was held by 2 sections). I am posthumously awarded the V.C.

On Wednesday I did some more painting at the baths. It was perishing cold, but I went for a swim for the first time.

Thursday – more painting, more swimming.

Friday – more painting, but it was too cold to swim.

Saturday – Mr Cox's car (a Wolseley 9) had a hole in the exhaust pipe, which I helped him to mend. He gave me some tea at his house, and then we went for a ride to see if it was all right. It was.

Today it is raining like anything, and I am reading the lesson in Chapel tonight. I must fly and prepare it.

P.S. I enclose an invitation to Speech Day. I have been working night shifts and overtime all this week.

* * *

Sunday June 10th '45

Thanks for your letter cards. I will find out the mileage and age of the three-wheeler at the earliest opportunity. Last Monday I went down to the baths and we worked out a Rota for the swimming prefects.

On Tuesday the platoon and section competitions were held. All our sections beat all the School House sections in everything. It was a very easy win. We won the platoon competition easily as well. (I believe I told you I was taking the drill). My name will go on the platoon shield, which will be presented (theoretically to me) at speech day. Unfortunately however, I won't be there, unless I come back from London for the day. (There is no exam on the Saturday).

On Wednesday if I remember rightly, it poured with rain,

and I did some work at an Inter-BSc Paper. I have been doing extra work all this week at night or getting up early in the mornings.

On Thursday afternoon there was a match against R.A.F. Wittering. We lost, but I can't remember the score. I worked part of the afternoon, and watched the match for the remainder.

On Friday I was on duty at the baths, but I didn't go in as the water was very cold.

Yesterday I shot in the competition for the Fenwick shooting cup. You will probably be pleased to hear that by a stroke of astonishing luck I won it! I beat Lane (who was off form) by 1 point. I got 72 and he got 71. It's a wizard cup and stands about 1 foot high in its socks. It will be presented to my representative on Speech Day. Afterwards I went to the baths and stayed there all the afternoon. Again I didn't go in owing to the 'coolth' of the water.

Today nothing spectacular has happened at all except that it has been cold and showery all day. The weather all the week has been perfectly beastly.

The lime trees may just be out when Mum comes over. I hope the weather will be good.

If I am here for the General Inspection I will probably be riding one of the Corps motor bikes.

On Saturday I got my entry card for the exam.

I must apologise for this scruffy letter but I am not really 'in the mood' for letter writing at the moment.

Because I have to take my Inter B.Sc. exams in London, I will be staying in Waddon with Uncle Tom and Auntie Kitty. It's only a short train ride and then I can get the tube to Kensington for the exams. My cousins, Kathie and Ann are great fun and we will be able to play tennis or go for cycle rides when I'm not having to do exams. I could also meet Kathie near Fleet Street at Lunchtime, as she works for one of the big newspapers.

S Kensington Post Office

Wednesday 27th June 1945

Sorry I've been so long in writing, but I have been rushing hither and thither or swotting most of the time so I haven't had a chance till now. I tried to ring you up, but Trunks wouldn't answer.

Thanks for your letter. I don't go to Uppingham till <u>next</u> Monday.

I will catch a train on Saturday at 10.10 a.m. which gets to Oakham at 1.22.

I am having a jolly good time, and the exam to date has gone quite well. The first paper on Monday I may have hashed up, but as there is another paper on the same subject (Applied Maths) I hope to pick up on that. I think I have got on OK with the Pure Maths papers I took and the Physics on toast.

I have no exams this morning, but I will have an engineering drawing paper this afternoon.

Back at Oakham I went to a cocktail party at the Hills' on Friday night, and David and I had 11 cocktails in 2 hours. We were both tight, and Dave was sick that night and the following morning, but I was OK. I went to Purley ice rink twice, swimming once, and played tennis once.

Halfway through the exams in London, I had to come back to Uppingham for one in Rutland! It made things very complicated.

Sunday 8th July 1945

Thanks very much indeed for the letter. The exams this

week were all quite reasonable and I really revelled in them. The practical applied Maths was a gift, and may help to pull me through on the theory paper.

The exam at Uppingham was not very nice, but I think I managed OK. I cycled from Uppingham to Manton station left the bike and collected the suitcase in plenty of time to catch the 6.18 from Manton. I got a compartment to myself all the way to Peterborough and had to change stations. When I had trooped to Peterborough North I sank four cups of tea in the refreshment room. I got a seat in the crowded ex-refreshment car to London because people had thought it was taken. I had to wait ages for a train to Waddon but eventually got one at London Bridge. I didn't get to Waddon and to the house till midnight.

On Tuesday I roamed round London and went to Selfridges to see the Aluminium Exhibition. There were some lovely aero engines, one E.R.A. Racing car, a racing boat and stacks of aluminium furniture. They can actually dye the metal a wide range of colours. The dyes are permanent. There were also some lovely aluminium fabrics of a wide variety of colours. They were really lovely. A jolly good exhibition. In the evening Kathie, Ann and I went to the ice rink at Purley. They are both learning to skate very well.

On Wednesday I had Practical Physics, and in the evening I went to the pictures in Croydon to see 'Czarina'. It was a ridiculous film, but quite amusing.

On Thursday I took Practical Chemistry in the afternoon, and we went out for a cycle ride to Mitcham.

It was a lovely evening, and there were hundreds of midges and things about. We came back absolutely covered with them.

On Friday I took Practical applied Maths, went to a News Theatre in the afternoon, and then as it was a nice evening, we went up to Addington Woods and roamed about there.

On Saturday I caught the 10.15 from King's Cross, changed at Peterborough and arrived back at Oakham on the 1.22
I have done nothing spectacular at school this weekend except that Lane, Jacobs and I went to Mr and Mrs Cox's for dinner last night.

9. Looking forward to dinner with Mr. & Mrs. Cox

It was lovely. We had tomato soup, plaice, green peas, new potatoes etc., and raspberries, strawberries, lemon curd tart etc. etc. It was very nice indeed.
If you let me know how much cash I was given for expenses, I will send you the change and my accounts next week.
P.S. Election day was very quiet in London. No fights or anything, as far as I could see.

Not much longer till the end of term now and I'm feeling very happy about that, though it will be a bit of a wrench to say goodbye to this place — and all my chums, of course.

Sunday 15th July 1945

Thanks very much for the letter. I have made arrangements

at the Crown for Dad's stay. I have invited all those named for dinner on Saturday night, and they all say they will be delighted to accept, but since the Headmaster and his wife will have someone staying with them, they are not yet sure if they will be able to come. I have however, though with difficulty, booked dinner for 9 at the Crown. I can always cancel two dinners if Mr and Mrs Griffith can't come. I have explained carefully the reason for not sending a written invitation.

There is precious little news, except that I was misinformed as to the date of Higher Cert's starting. It doesn't start till tomorrow, and I have been feverishly swotting up formulae and things.

On Friday I helped at a Practical Chemistry exam for School Cert.

We have had a terrific heat wave here, and the baths are now at 74ºF. It's lovely in.

I have been swimming in heats for the swimming sports but without success.

We had a dorm feast last night at 1 a.m. D.B. Summer time, as the clocks were being put back, and I was utterly stodged. Incidentally we had the most spectacular thunder storm I have ever seen. It lasted 9 hours, and I took a photo of some lightening.

I apologise for this brief scrawl, but its nearly time for chapel.

Well, that's the end of School for me. The Higher Cert Exams are over and I can relax. Dad came over and we had a lovely dinner party at the 'Crown'. They managed to make a pigeon pie for us, which was absolutely delicious. I didn't realise I would be quite so sad when I caught the 9.02 back to Birmingham for the last time.

When I first left home to go away to school the War was just starting. Now I'm leaving school to go home again the War's finished — in Europe, anyway. With Germany beaten Japan won't hold out for much longer. The lights are on again, which is wonderful, but we will have rationing for ages, I suppose. It's not clear what will happen about my military service. Everything is in the melting pot.

For me, it's exciting to look forward to working in a car factory as an apprentice. I've already managed to buy an old Ford engine for ten bob. I got it home in Dad's wheelbarrow, then took it to bits and rebuilt it in the garage.

Postscript

September 1945

A new chapter in my life starts today, 10th September 1945. This reminds me of another big event for me — a ride in an Albion coach to a new school as an evacuee. But now I'm on a different sort of bus, a Birmingham Corporation Daimler double-decker, a journey of about thirty minutes on the number 11 Outer Circle route. I'm travelling on the section from King's Heath to Drews Lane in Ward End. That's the home of Wolseley Cars where I will be working in the factory and the technical offices as an Engineering Apprentice. But I suppose I could get moved to another of the Nuffield factories in Birmingham, Oxford or Coventry.

It's difficult to guess what the next few years hold for me, but I'm really looking forward to this period of 'further education'. And then what? Dad was fond of saying, "never put any limit on your ambition", so I'll just have to wait and see what happens, won't I?

Author's Note

My parents came originally from Ryhope, a coalmining village just south of Sunderland in the northeast of England. My father, Norman Iley, was the second son of the village chemist. There were seven children who survived infancy. In descending age there were five sons (Bob, Norman, Tom, Walter and Fred) followed by two daughters (Edith and Ethel). My mother, Winifred Bowman, was the daughter of the senior fitter at the coalmine — always referred to as 'the pit'. She had an elder brother, Cecil, and a younger sister, Betty.

Norman and Winnie were married on 3rd September 1924 and started their married life in Blyth, a small seaport north of the Tyne, where my father worked at the Midland Bank (later absorbed by HSBC). My mother returned to Ryhope for my birth. I was born on 24th September 1928, in the Bowman's end terrace house, which came with Grandad's job at the pit. Two of my godparents were from within the family — Uncle Tom Iley and Auntie Betty Bowman.

My stay in the northeast did not last long; at the age of six weeks we all went to live in lodgings in Handsworth, Birmingham, as my father had just been sent by the bank to work in their branch at Bennett's Hill, in the city centre. Soon afterwards we moved to Burman Road, Shirley, on the south side of Birmingham. Successive postings took us to Lincoln, where I started school, first at a kindergarten, then at Lincoln Grammar School. In 1935 we moved to Avondale Road, Croydon, where I attended Coombe Hill House School. Finally, towards the end of the 1930's, we were back in Birmingham again, where we lived in a semi-detached house at 64 Shutlock Lane in Moseley. This had a large garden and — what bliss — a stream running along the left hand side. Although these were anxious times with Germany's menace as a black cloud on the horizon, this went largely unnoticed by young boys like me. I was more concerned about looking for sticklebacks in the stream and conker fights at my school, Woodroughs in Moseley.

Just before the outbreak of war, in August 1939, we went on holiday to Felpham on the South Coast along with my parents' great friends, Eddie Edwards — Dad's colleague from the Midland Bank — his wife Linda and their two daughters, Paula and Mariane. As I was an only child and we lived so far away from my many cousins, Paula and Mariane had already been 'family' for me for much of my young life.

After the bombings of cities in the Spanish civil war, my parents were worried that Birmingham would be a prime target for air raids in the coming conflict. So, after arguments and soul-searching, they planned to send me away for safety. My parents stayed behind in Birmingham, braving the Blitz while they got on with their wartime lives — though we were reunited during school holidays.

The war ended and years passed. I married, had a career in industry and became a family man. My father died in 1975, my mother in 1988. They left behind a great deal of memorabilia that I inherited. The daunting task of sorting out their 'treasures' was continually put off year after year until, eventually, my wife and I downsized to an apartment with very little storage space. This forced the issue and it was only then that a surprising cache of correspondence came to light. It contained every letter that I had written home during the time I was away during WW II from 2nd September 1939 until 15th July 1945. There were around a hundred and ninety altogether and this memoir is based on that original source material. It reveals the self-centred arrogance of an only child, together with curiosity, hypochondria, unquestioning patriotism and a number of obsessions. I hope that he's learned a lot since then, so please don't judge him too harshly.

Chronos Books is a historical non-fiction imprint. Chronos publishes real history for real people; bringing to life historical people, places and events in an imaginative, easy-to-digest and accessible way. We want writers of historical books, from ancient times to the Second World War, that will add to our understanding of people and events rather than being a dry textbook; history that passes on its stories to a generation of new readers.